A SHORT HISTORICAL SURVEY OF THE MUSIC OF UPPER INDIA

A SHORT HISTORICAL SURVEY OF THE MUSIC OF UPPER INDIA

(A REPRODUCTION OF A SPEECH DELIVERED BY PANDIT V. N. BHATKHANDE AT THE FIRST ALL-INDIA MUSIC CONFERENCE, BARODA IN 1916.)

PANDIT VISNU NARAYANA BHATAKHANDE

GYAN

Published by

GYAN

Gyan Publishing House
5, Ansari Road
Daryaganj, New Delhi-110002
Phone: 011-47034999, 9811692060
E-mail: books@gyanbooks.com

Distribution Network
gyanbooks.com
India, USA, Canada, UK, Australia, France

ISBN: 978-81-212-7095-3 (PB)

First Published, 1934

2nd Impression 2024

Printed at: Gyan Press, Delhi.

A SHORT HISTORICAL SURVEY OF THE MUSIC OF UPPER INDIA

Author: PANDIT VISNU NARAYANA BHATAKHANDE

पंडित विष्णु नारायण भातखंडे

A SHORT HISTORICAL SURVEY OF THE MUSIC OF UPPER INDIA

(A reproduction of a Speech delivered by Pandit V. N. Bhatkhande at the First All-India Music Conference, Baroda, in 1916.)

YOUR Highness, Mr. President, brother members of the Conference, Ladies and Gentlemen,

A satisfactory feature of the Renaissance of Indian culture and Indian ideals, which characterises the intellectual activity in India of the present day, is the attention that is paid to the revival of our ancient music. The keen interest evinced by the present generation in the preservation and further progress of this national heirloom has materialised itself broadly speaking, in two different aspects. On the one hand, one notices the movement of learned scholars from all parts of India meeting in national conferences with a view to focus attention on and co-ordinate the results of research grappling with the technical side of the question; such as for instance, the working out of a system of uniform and adequate notation; the systematising of the *rāgas* at present sung in the northern part of the country, so as to make the same easy of instruction and assimilation, and so forth. On the other hand, one welcomes the growth of numerous music clubs and schools of music,—and with it the facilities offered for a serious and thorough-going study of the art,—and its gradual introduction into our homesteads.

Both these aspects are complementary of each other, neither is complete without the other. The learned but dry-as-dust disquisitions of our theorists would be fruitless waste of time if they did not succeed in evoking some interest on the part of the public in the art; while the Gayan Samaj would be a deplorably shaky superstructure without the firm foundation of the science.

We shall leave the Gayan Samaj movement to grow and prosper along its own lines, and meanwhile turn our attention to one issue connected with the scientific side of the question. We are now fully alive to the fact that no study of a science is complete without a study of the history of the science. It will, therefore, not be amiss to cast a retrospective glance in the direction of the past history of Hindusthani Sangit, so far as the scanty material at present available will permit. There is no dearth of material, it must be confessed; but the specially rich harvest of the ancient literature on music serves, for lack of interest at the present time, only to burden the bookshelves of our libraries; and until these works are made available to the public after having been carefully edited, our knowledge of the history of this art must needs remain defective and unconnected. For this reason I crave the indulgence of the audience.

To the Hindu mind, the sister arts of Vocal Music, Instrumental Music, and Dancing are so intimately connected with each other, that the term "Sangit" was used by ancient writers to include all the three together, although, I need hardly point out, strictly speaking, it is applicable only to the first, namely, Vocal Music. I do not propose to deal with Instrumental Music or Dancing here, and it should be understood that I use the word Sangit in the *restricted* connotation of *Vocal Music.* I shall further circumscribe my thesis by confining my attention mainly to the system which is prevalent in the Northern part of the country.

You are all aware probably, that there are, at the present day, current in India two different systems of music which are perfectly independent of each other; I mean of course the Hindusthani and the Karnatik systems. These two great schools have existed in the country for many centuries past, and the chief difference between them two lies in their two perfectly independent *shuddha* or primary scales. Our present Hindusthani system is based on what is commonly called the Bilāval scale, which very nearly corresponds with the European scale of C. The *shuddha* scale of the Southern system is called the Kanakāngi scale, which will indeed sound extremely odd to our ears, but that it exists and forms the foundation of the Southern system cannot be denied. It will be, as I shall mention later on, a very interesting problem in the history of Indian Music to determine how and when the Northern musicians first obtained or adopted the Bilāval scale as their *shuddha* scale. The reasons why I do not propose to include the history of Southern music in my remarks on this occasion are first, that my own acquaintance with the Southern music system is not far from superficial; and secondly, that in my opinion the musicians of the Southern presidency are not so handicapped in their progress as we Northerners here are. It is commonly known that, comparatively speaking, the music system of Southern India is much more developed and accurate than that of the northern part of the country, and has a well preserved *Sāstric* tradition. I understand it is capable of being studied and taught with the help of regular text-books. It is said that many educated people in Southern India make a systematic study of the science and art of music and thus to a certain extent are able to exercise a healthy control over the professional artists, who, besides, are not so hopelessly illiterate and ignorant as their brethren in the north. With us Northerners, on the other hand, the situation is indeed deplorable, as we are here, more or less, at the mercy of the ignorant and narrow-minded professionals. I may add that during the last decade or two things are changing their gloomy aspect and are somewhat brightening up but the progress is extremely slow and unsystematic. I do not mean to say that we have absolutely nothing like a basis of a music system of our own, but it cannot be denied that we have lost touch with the *Sāstric* traditions and have been for some time past at least drifting away. It is true that we find nowadays Hindusthani music being taught in some of our schools and private classes; but in the absence of any thing like a uniform and intelligent system, the tuition given there becomes somewhat haphazard and unsystematic. At least it does not seem to come up to a very high standard. The condition of the music of Northern India, therefore, needs prompt and proper consideration.

The most convenient method of dealing with the history of Hindusthani music appears to be to divide the subject into three distinct periods, *viz.,* (1) the Hindu period, (2) the Mahomedan period, and (3) the British period. Each of these periods may again be sub-divided, if necessary, into two divisions, *viz.,* (1) the earlier and (2) the later. The Mahomedans came into contact with this country as a ruling nation in the 11th century A.D., and remained here as such till about the end of the 18th century, after which date, the country passed under the domination of our present rulers, the British. This historical fact enables us at once to fix the boundaries of the three periods necessary for us. The Hindu period according to this classification begins, from the Vedic times and extends right up to the end of the 10th century A.D.

I do not propose to discuss the music history of the Hindu period on this occasion and do not, therefore, think it necessary to make any lengthy remarks about the literature of that period, but it may not be out of place to point out here in passing that there is still a lot of research work remaining to be done in connection with the history of that period. As far as the present state of our knowledge goes, the only work of any historical importance, yet discovered, that is likely to throw some useful light on the conditions of music in those times is the *Natya Shastra* of Bharata, a writer believed to belong to the third or fourth century A.D. That work again, as its very title indicates, is a treatise on the ancient Hindu Drama, and deals with music only incidentally. It says absolutely nothing about *rāgas* and *rāginis,* but deals, in the only three chapters it devotes to music with the *shrutis, gramas, murchhanas,* and *jatis* of the ancient Hindu Music. The complete absence in the work of any reference to *rāgas* and *rāginis* is no doubt remarkable, and disappointing too, and it is sought to be explained by some modern scholars by saying that in the time of the author the term *rāga* itself had not come into existence at all. This will, of course, be a debatable point and we shall not enter into its discussion here. We are constantly told that our music has had for its source the great *Sāma Veda,* a work some three or four thousand years old, but no scholar either ancient or modern seems to have yet successfully established an intelligible and satisfactory connection between Sama music and that of the succeeding writers. We have some works like the *Shikshās* and *Pratishākhyas,* but they do not carry us very far. If we leave the Vedic times and come to those of the Epics and ancient Dramas, we have ample evidence that music had attained a very high position in society and that it was capable of being regularly studied and taught both as a science and an art; but as to what it actually was, we have absolutely no reliable information, because none of the music treatises of that period are at present available. Thus we see that barring the *Nātya Shāstra* of Bharata, we are very poorly equipped in the matter of reliable records for a faithful history of the early Hindu period. Between Bharata and the advent of the Mahomedans into the country, there is another gap of some seven or eight centuries. This is supposed to have been the golden age of our music. With regard to it Capt. Day in his *Music of Southern India,* at page 3, tells us that "the most flourishing age of Indian music was during the period of the native princes, a little before the Mahomedan conquest. With the advent of the Mahomedans its decline commenced. Indeed, it is wonderful that it survived at all." As no treatise on the music of that period has survived, we are deprived of the only means, by which we could get any idea of the condition of music in those times. The above remarks of Capt. Day apply, strictly speaking, only to the music of Hindusthana proper. As regards the Southern music he goes on to say : "Owing to the South of India having been less disturbed by internal commotion and having been more subject to Hindu rule than either the Dekkan or the Northern provinces, the science of music would seem to have been maintained and cultivated long after the original art had been lost in the north." It is not only true that we, in the North, have come to lose our ancient, works on the science of music, but we can hardly boast of having duly preserved any of our old Sanskrit compositions either. But it may here be objected that we have even at this day some *Prabandhas* like those of the eminent poet and musician Jayadeva of the 12th century A.D. I do not deny that we have preserved these. But is that enough, having regard to the fact that we claim to be the oldest musical nation in the world ? Then again, the question will arise, do we sing even one of these *Prabandhas* in the original *rāga* and *tāla* of

Jayadeva ? On this point the remarks of that great oriental scholar Sir William Jones will be found most interesting. He says : "When I first read the songs of Jayadeva, who has prefixed to each of them *(Prabandhas)* the name of the mode in which it was anciently sung, I had hopes of procuring the original music; but the Pandits of the South referred me to those of the West and the Brahmans of the West would have sent me to those of the North, while they. I mean those of Nepaul and Kashmere declared that they had no ancient music, but imagined that the notes of the Gita Govinda must exist, if anywhere, in one of the Southern provinces where the poet was born." Now, is this not really very funny having regard to the fact that Jayadeva never had anything to do with the South, he having been born in and flourished at Beerbhum in Bengal?

In tracing the history of the music of Northern India in the Mahomedan period, the first work that forces itself on our notice is the one entitled *Rāga Tarangini* written by one Lochanakavi. The date of the work as given by the author is as follows :—

भुजवसुदशमितशाके श्रीमब्दल्लालसेनराज्यादौ।
वर्षैकषष्टिभोगे मुनयस्त्वासन् विशाखायाम् ।।

Here the expression भुजवसुदशमितशाके gives us the Shaka year 1082 corresponding to A.D. 1162. There seems to be, however, some discrepancy in the enumeration of the astronomical details. Lochanakavi refers in the work to two famous previous writers, namely, Jayadeva and Vidyāpati. As I have not with me a complete copy of the *Rdga Tarangini,* and the only material I rely upon in making these remarks is an extract purporting to be a copy of the *svara* and *rāga adhyāyas* of the work, kindly lent to me by a friend in Upper India, I must content myself by quoting a portion of his letter covering the extract. "The *Rāga Tarangini* purports to be a treatise on music, but 62 out of the 100 pages to which it extends are devoted to the prosody of songs composed by a poet of local fame named Vidyāpati in the Maithili dialect of the Hindi language. The songs are quoted by way of examples of *deshi rāgas.* Each quotation is preceded by a *shloka* or two stating the number of *mātrās* contained in and other particulars regarding the metre in which the song is composed. These quotations are introduced as follows:—

मार्गदेशीविभेदेन गीतं तु द्विविधं मतम्।
मार्गास्तु गंधर्वादिगीतगतयः। देश्यश्च तत्तद्रागाश्रितास्तास्तास्तत्तद्देशगीतगतयः
इह तु मार्गाभावान्नोदाहृताः अग्रे तु क्कचिदुदाहर्तव्याः। देश्यामपि स्वदेशीयत्वात्
प्रथमं मिथिलापभ्रंशभाषया श्रीविद्यापतिकविनिवद्धास्तास्ता मैथिलंगीतगतयः प्रदर्श्यंते।।

Then follows the pedigree of the poet Vidyāpati. (I wish my friend had copied it.) Next a few lines about the elements of prosody and then the lengthy series of Vidyāpati's songs and some by the author of the treatise himself whose name is Lochanakavi. These songs are composed in metres which are given the names of the *rāgas* and *rāginis.* I give only one specimen here as I do not believe that the songs can be of much use to you.

अथ देशाखनामरागिपणी। अत्र तु जयदेवदेशाखः, देशदेशाख इति भैदद्वयम्।
जयदेवदेशाखे तु श्रीजयदेवः। स्तनविनिहितमपि हारमुदारं। सा मनुते कृश–
तनुरतिभारम् ध्रु.। राधिकाविरहे तव केशव इत्यादि सुप्रसिद्धम्।

"There are only two cases where Jayadeva is quoted."

देशदेशाखे तु तन्नामकमेव छंदः। तल्लक्षणं
चतुर्मात्रागणानां तु कलाहीनं चतुष्टयं।।
चतुष्टयं कलाप्रासं तद्वा प्रतिपदार्धके।
सप्तमे सप्तमे वर्णे विरामो विगतध्रुवम्।।

देशदेशाख इत्याख्यछंदस्तत्र तुतान्नयेत्।
उदाहरणम्।
मानपरिहरहे करूवचन मोरा
मारमनोभवहे धरूसरन मोरा
न करन करहे मोहि विमुख आजे
अपरूवये मेहे (?) पुन मेल समाजे
कमलवदनिहे करू आकमदाने
विनएकेनहिहे (sic) जगॅते जए माने।
इति विद्यापतिः।।
मम तु।
निरज नयनि गिरिराजउरोजे
सौहॅन करहेह किए मुखसरोजे
अमि अँ माषलिहे मोहि विनयहानी।

"And then eight more couplets of the author's own composition. Such songs fill by far the larger part of the treatise. As I have said before, the treatise begins with two third-rate मंगलाचरण *shlokas.* Then follows the pedigree of the author ending with the following *shloka :*

किंचित्समाहृत्य कुतश्रिद्न्यत् स्वयं च संपाद्य पदप्रबंधम्।
वितन्यते लोचननामधेयद्विजेन सा रागतरंगिणीयम्।।

"The author then goes on to say that there were 16,000 *rāgas* and that they were sung by Gopis before Krishna, but of these only 36 are well-known now. These are enumerated in the *shlokas* which are commonly met with in most treatises on music. The *sholaks* begin with :

भैरवः कौशिकश्चैवहिंदोलो दीपकस्तथा।
श्रीरागो मेघरागश्च षडेते हनुमन्मताः।।

The next ten pages contain *shlokas* enumerating the *rāginis* of these *rāgas* and giving their देवतात्मक pictures. The following is a specimen of the *shlokas* :

अथ मेघरागः।
असितकमलकान्तिः पीतवासाः स्मितास्यः
समदयुवतियूथान्तर्गतश्चंद्रहृत्कः।
वितरति किल लोके जीवनं यः स्वभावात्
जयति समुपास्यश्चातकैर्मेघरागः।।

"I give only one specimen here as I think you will not care to have such descriptions. I thought you would care more to have the नादात्मकस्वरूप of each of the *ragas,* but they are not given in the work."

As to the verse giving the date of the work, my friend adds, "as to the *Aryā* giving the date of the author, the first half would show that the work was composed in Shaka 1082, but how the Munis that are now in Maghas could be in Vishakhas I do not understand." Raja Sir S. M. Tagore in his *"Universal History of Music,"* pp. 77-8 ascribes the poets Jayadeva and Vidyāpati to the 12th and 14th centuries respectively. He further tells us that Vidyāpati flourished at the court of Raja Shiva Singh of Tirhut in Behar. Now, if this statement is correct then Lochanakavi who quotes from Jayadeva and Vidyāpati evidently could not have written his work in Shaka 1082 or A.D. 1162. I think the determination of the date of this work would be a very interesting problem for our research scholars to undertake.

Whatever the date of the treatise may be, the work appears to me very remarkable even from the point of view of practical music. The स्वरसंज्ञाप्रकरण of the book, for instance, will be found most interesting and instructive. I shall quote it here :

स्वस्वशेषश्रुतिं त्यक्तवा सदा रिषभधैवतै।
गीयेते गुणिभिः सवैस्तदा तौ कोमलौ मतौ।।
गृहणति मध्यमस्यापि गांधारः प्रथमां श्रुतिम्।
यदा तदा जनैरेष तीव्र इत्यभिघीयते।।
द्वितीयामपि चेदेवं तदा तीव्रतरः स्मृतः।
तृतीयामपि चेदेवं तदा तीव्रतमः स्मृतः।
चतुर्थीमपि चेदेवमतितीव्रतमः स्मृतः।।
अतितीव्रतमो गस्तु सारंगे परिगीयते।
षड्जस्य च निषादश्चेद् गृहणति प्रथमां श्रुतिम्।।
तदा संगीतिभिः सोऽपि तीव्र इत्यभिधीयते।
द्वितीयामपि चेदेवं तदा तीव्रतरः स्मृतः।।
तृतीयामपि चेदेवं तदा तीव्रतमः स्मृतः
षड्जस्य द्वे श्रुती गृहण्न् निषादः काकली स्मृतः
तीव्रतरे निषादैव गेया सैव विचक्षणैः।।

(See pp. 2-3.)

A mere glance at this *Svaraprakarana* is enough to show that this work is one of the northern authorities and that its *shuddha* scale is no other than that of the modern *Kāphi rāga.* Lochanakavi lays down twelve *janaka melas* or parent *thatas* and then classifies his *janya rāgas* under them. His twelve *thātas* are :—

भैरवी टोडिका तद्वत् गौरी कर्णाट एव च
केदार इमनस्तद्वत् सारंगो मेघरागकः।
धनाश्रीः पूरवी किंच मुखारीदीपकस्तथा
एतेषामेवसंस्थाने सर्वे रागा व्यवस्थिताः।
तत्र यद्रागसंस्थाने ये ये रागा व्यवस्थिताः।
यथा यद्रागसंस्थानं तत्तथैव वदाम्यहम।
इति संस्थानसंज्ञा प्रकरणम्

(1) भैरवी

शुद्धाः सप्तस्वरा रम्या वादनीयाः प्रयत्नतः।
तेन वादनमात्रेण भैरवी जायते शुभा।।
अन्ये तु भैरवी रागे धैवतं कोमलं विदुः।
तदशुद्धं यतस्ताध्क् नायंरागोऽनुरंजकः।।

(2) टोडी

शुद्धाः सप्त स्वराः कार्या रिधौ तेषु च कोमलौ।
टोडी सुरागिणी ज्ञेया ततो गायकनायकैः।।

(3) गौरी

एवं सतिच गांधारो द्वे श्रुती मध्यमस्य चेत्।
गृह्णाति काकली निः स्यात् तदा गौरी प्रवर्तते।।

(See pp. 3-4.)

I have quoted the last four *shlokas* here with a view to enable you to fix correctly the *shuddha* scale of the *Rāga Tarangini.* The short *Rāga-dhyāya* of *Tarangini* is also interesting but it is not necessary to insert it here. A careful examination of this work yields the following six important historical points:

(1) That the names of the *svaras* and *rāgas* are purely northern.

(2) That the twelve *thātas* are almost all northern.

(3) That the author used only 12 *svaras* in describing his *rāgas.*

(4) That many of the *rāga lakshanas* in the book will be useful even now.

(5) That all music was confined to the *shadja-grāma* only.

(6) That the method of obtaining *rāgas* from the *murchhanas* and *jātis* had become obsolete.

We shall leave the *Tarangini* aside for tne present and proceed to consider the condition of our music during the twelfth and thirteenth centuries A.D., that is to say, during the period preceding the reign of Sultan Alla-ud-din of Delhi. This period is said to be one of the most important periods in Indian History, but unfortunately for us, this is again a period for which we have nothing like reliable music records. Historians tell us that during the early days of the Mahomedan conquest our music suffered very badly at the hands of the conquerors. Capt. Willards in his book, *"A Treatise on the Music of Hindusthan"* at p. 106 says :— "The conquest of Hindusthan by the Mahomedan princes forms a most important epoch in the history of its music. From this time we may date the decline of all arts and sciences purely Hindu, for the Mahomedans were no great patrons to learning, and the more bigoted of them were not only great iconoclasts, but discouragers of the learning of the country. The progress of the theory of music once arrested, its decline was speedy, although the practice which contributed to the entertainment of the princes and nobles, continued until the time of Mahomed Shah, after whose reign history is pregnant with facts replete with dismal scenes. But the practice of so fleeting and perishable a science as that of a succession of sounds, without a knowledge of the theory to keep it alive, or any mode to record it on paper, dies with the professor." These remarks of the learned writer need not surprise us at all. It is not in India alone that the Mahomedan invaders distinguished themselves by their ruthlessness towards music. The history of Persian music after the conquest of Persia by the Musulmans reflects a similar state of things there. It is said, "when the Mahomedans conquered Persia, Saad the son of Abu Wakhas wrote to Omar, the second Caliph after Mahomed to be allowed to send a number of Persian works on music to him. Omar's simple answer was to throw them into the waters as useless to the Faith. The order was so completely carried out by the burning of all books, that the only musical work now known to exist in the Persian language is one entitled 'Heela Imaeli' mentioned in a catalogue appended to Mr. Fraser's history of Nadirshah." The Persians, as we all know, had a very ancient civilization and as a civilized nation they possessed a regular music system of their own before the conquest of their country by the Mahomedans in the seventh century.

Sultan Alla-ud-din, who ruled at Delhi about the close of the thirteenth century, seems to have been very fond of music and gave great encouragement to the art. It was at his court that the famous Persian poet and musician Amir Khosru flourished. Amir Khosru has left a permanent mark on the music of Hindusthan, inasmuch as it was he who introduced into the country the *quavali* mode of singing for the first time. He is also credited with having introduced here several of our modern *rāgas* like *Zilaph, Sāzagiri, Sarpardā* and others. Among the several interesting stories told about this wonderful genius Khosru, there is one which will strike us as of some historical importance and that is his musical combat with and defeat of the great Southern musician Gopal Nayak. We are at once led to enquire first, whether Gopal Nayak was really a contemporary of Amir Khosru and secondly, whether he went all the way to Delhi to have a combat with him. In the absence of conclusive evidence in the form of authentic records it will be impossible of course, to determine these questions with the necessary amount of certainty; but it will be useful to carefully consider some historical facts that are now available to us. Thus, we find that in the first quarter of the 15th century (about the year A.D. 1425) there lived and flourished at the court of Raja Devaraja of Vijayanagar an eminent musician and Pandit by name Kallinatha the son of Lakshmidhara. Kallinatha wrote a great commentary on the *Sangita Ratnākara* of Sharangadeva. In his commentary on the *tola adhyāya,* when speaking about a tala called *"kudukka,"* Kallinatha refers to Gopal Nayak as follows :—

कुडुक्कतालस्तु गोपालनायकेन
रागकदंबैरेवगुप्तवदप्रयुक्तः।।

(vide p. 433, Anandashram Edition of *Sangita Ratnakara).* From this it clearly follows that Gopal Nayak had attained a great reputation in Kallinatha's time and that he was looked upon as an important authority on matters musical. If it be conceded then that Gopal Nayak preceded Kallinatha by about a century or so, there is nothing to prevent the inference that he may have flourished about the beginning of the 14th century, and thus may have been the contemporary of both Sultan Alla-ud-din and his court musician Amir Khosru. As to the other question whether Gopal Nayak went to Delhi, we have the following fairly reliable information which throws some light on the question.

"It is related by Mahomedan historians of the period that when Dacca was invaded by Alla-ud-din in A.D. 1294 and the conquest of the South of India was completed in A.D. 1310 by his Mogul general Malik Kafur, music was in such a flourishing condition that all the musicians and their Hindu preceptors were taken with the royal armies and settled in the North." (Raja Sir S. M. Tagore's *History of Universal Music,* p. 54). Col. P. T. French, in his paper on *"The Indian musical instruments,"* read before the Royal Irish Academy, says the same thing in the following words :—There are many Sanskrit as well as Telegu, Canarese and Tamil works on music still in existence. Indeed, in the South of India music appears to have been maintained and cultivated as a science long after it had ceased as such in the North. Mahomedan historians of the period relate that when the Dekkan was invaded by Alla-ud-din Tughaluk in A.D. 1294 and the conquest of the South of India completed by the Mogul general Malik Kafur, several years afterwards, the profession of music was found to be in a condition so far advanced of the North, that singers, male and female, musicians and their Brahmin instructors were taken with the royal armies and settled in the North." Malik Kafur invaded the Dekkan about the year A.D. 1310 and overthrew the Yadava dynasty of Devagiri (the modern Daulatabad). I confess we have no means to know definitely where Gopal Nayak lived and flourished but if he was attached to one of the Yadava courts, which is not unlikely, it is quite conceivable that he was among the learned music Pandits of the South who went to Delhi with the royal armies of Sultan Alla-ud-din. About the actual combat supposed to have taken place between Gopal Nayak and Amir Khosru Capt. Willard says as follows :—

"It is related that when Gopal visited the court of Delhi he sang that species of composition called *Gita,* the beauty of which style enunciated by the powerful and harmonious voice of so able a performer could not meet with competition. At this the Monarch caused Umeer Khosrow to remain hid under his throne, whence he could hear the musician unknown to him. The latter endeavoured to remember the style and on a subsequent day sang Quoal and Turana in imitation of it which surprised Gopal and fraudulently deprived him of a portion of his due honour" (vide p. 107, *Treatise on the Music of Hindusthan).*

At this distance of time it will be impossible, of course, to obtain any more convincing or reliable information on the point but the story of the combat seems to be too familiarly known to be set aside as a pure myth or invention.

While speaking about the condition of our music in the 13th and the 14th centuries, and particularly about Devagiri and its rulers the Yadava princes, we cannot omit to take notice of that greatest of our available musical authorities which has never ceased to inspire awe and reverence in the minds of all our music scholars of the last six hundred years or so. I am referring, of course, to the *Sangita Ratnākara* of Pandit Sharangadeva. The date of the work is easily fixed because the author in the very opening verses thereof describes his ancestors and patrons in the following terms :—

अस्ति स्वस्तिगृहं वंशः श्रीमान्काश्मोरसंभवः।
ऋषेर्वर्षगणाज्जातः कीर्तिक्षालितदिङ्मुखः।।2।।

यज्वभिर्धर्मधीधुर्यैर्वेदसागरपारगैः।
यो द्विजेंद्रैरलंचक्रे ब्रह्ममिभूगतैरिव।।3।।

तत्राभूभ्दास्करप्रख्यो भास्करस्तेजसां निधिः।
अलंकर्तुं दक्षिणाशां यश्चक्रे दक्षिणायनम्।।4।।

तस्याभूत्तनयः प्रभूतविनयः श्रोसोढलः प्रौढधी-
र्यन श्रीकरणप्रबुद्धविभवं भूवल्लभं भिल्लमम्।।

आराध्याखिललोकशोकशमनी कीर्तिः समासादिता।
जैत्रे जैत्रपदं न्यधायि महती श्रीसिंघणे श्रीरपि।।5।।

From these verses it dearly appears that Sharangadeva's grandfather originally belonged to Kashmere and that for some reason or other he subsequently travelled down to the South and settled in the Dekkan. We are not distinctly told here if the learned gentleman was a great musician also. Bhaskar Pandit's son Sodhala, it appears, entered later on the service of the Yadava kings Bhillama and Singhana. Dr. Sir R. G. Bhandarkar in his *Early History of the Dekkan* gives us the names of the later Rajas of the Yadava dynasty of Devagiri among which those of Bhillama (1187-1191 A.D.) and Singhana (1210-1217 A.D.) will be of importance to us, because they will enable us to fix the time when Sharangadeva's grandfather Bhaskara arrived at Devagiri. Among his predecessors, Sharangadeva mentions the names of the following authorities on music :

सदाशिवः शिवा ब्रह्मा भरतः कश्यपो मुनिः।
मतंगो याष्टिको दुर्गाशक्तिः शार्दूलकोहलौ ॥15॥

विशाखिलो दन्तिलश्च कम्बलोऽश्वतरस्तथा।
वायुर्विश्वावसू रंभार्जुननारदतुंबराः ॥16॥

आंजनेयो मातृगुप्तो रावणो नंदिकेश्वरः।
स्वातिर्गुणो बिंदुराजः क्षेत्रराजश्च राहलः ॥17॥

रुद्रटो नान्यभूपालो भोजभूवल्लभस्तथा।
परमर्दी च सोमेशो जगदेकमहीपतिः ॥18॥

व्याख्यातारो भारतीये लोल्लटोभ्दटशंकुकाः।
भट्टाभिनवगुप्तश्च श्रीमत्कीर्तिधरोऽपराः ॥19॥

अन्ये च बहवः पूर्वे ये संगीतविशारदाः।
अगाधबोधमंथेन तेषां मतपयोनिधिम् ॥
निर्मथ्य श्रीशाङ्र्गदेवः सारोद्धारमिमं व्यधात् ॥20॥

It is not to be supposed that all these persons named here were music writers actually and that Pandit Sharangadeva had access to their works, but there is no doubt that in the time of the Pandit there were many Granthas available from which he could draw his material. A reference to the *"Early History of India"* by Vincent Smith will give us the dates of Bhoja,

Someshvara, and Paramardi as A.D. 1053, 1183 and 1208 respectively, which shows that the kings were really the predecessors of Sharangadeva. Dr. H. H. Wilson in his *"Theatre of the Hindus,"* Vol. I, p. 22 (third edition), says :— "The Sangit Ratnakara treats more especially of singing and dancing than that of dramatic literature. It furnishes, however, some curious notices of the theatrical representation and gesture. It is the work of Sharangadeva, the son of Sodhala the son of Bhaskara, a Kashmerian pandit, who sought fortunes in the South. His grandson was patronized by a prince named Sinhaladeva but of what time or place he does not inform us. It is clear, however, that he wrote between the 12th and the 15th century (A.D.) as he names Bhoja among his predecessors in the science; and a comment on his own work was written by Kallinatha, by the desire of Praudha or Pratap Deva, King of Vijayanagara from A.D. 1456 to 1477."

I think it is now fairly established that the *Sangita Ratnākara* of Sharangadeva came to be written somewhere about the latter half of the 13th century A.D. Although this work is looked upon to-day as the first and foremost of our musical authorities, it must be noted that its music is not clearly understood in any part of the country. This statement will, no doubt, sound somewhat paradoxical but the fact remains that there is not a single scholar in India, at present, who has been successful in solving the *rāgas* elaborately described in *Ratnākara.* Nay ! even the question, whether *Ratnākara* is a northern or a southern authority, has yet to be satisfactorily solved. Some scholars seem inclined to believe that it is a northern authority, and even venture to go further and assert that the present Hindusthani system of music is not far removed from that of Sharangadeva himself. But it must also be remarked here that they have not yet produced anything like convincing evidence in support of their claims. The Southern Pandits, on the other hand, point to the technical language and *rāgas* of *Ratnākara* and say that they are undeniably southern. They also draw our attention to the fact that almost all the Sanskrit writers of the last five centuries have, rightly or wrongly, continued to cite *Ratnakara* as they own authority, and have even gone the length of comparing their own *melas* (modes) and *rāgas* with those given in the book. There will, no doubt, appear some force in their argument, but it must be stated here also that even the southern writers do not seem to have clearly followed the music of *Ratnākara.* I think it will not be irrelevant here to give you an idea as to how the Southern writers refer to Sharangadeva's *Ratnākara* in their own works. Thus, Pandit Rama Amatya in his *Svaramelakalānidhi* says :—

एते षड्जादयः सप्त स्वराः शुद्धाः प्रकीर्तिताः ।
विकृताश्चैव सप्तैवेत्येवं सर्वे चतुर्दश ।।

ननु रत्नाकरे शार्ङ्गदेवेन विकृताः स्वराः ।
द्वादशोक्ताः कर्थ तेतु सप्तैव कथितास्त्वया ।।

सत्यं लक्षणतो भेदो द्वादशनामपीष्यते ।
शुद्धेभ्यस्तत्र भेदस्तु सप्तानामेव लक्षितः ।।"

X X X

शुद्धसप्तस्वरैयुक्तो मुखारीमेलको भवैत् ।।
अस्मिन्मेले मुखारी च ग्रामरागाश्च केचन ।

संमतः शुद्ध इत्येष शार्ङ्गदेवविपश्चितः ।
शुद्धौ च षड्जरिषभौ शुद्धाश्च मपधास्तथा ।।

गांधारोंऽतरसंज्ञश्च कांकलाख्यनिषादकः ।
एतावत्स्वरसंयुक्तो हिजूजीभेलकोमवेत् ।।

हिजूज्याद्या भवंत्यत्र ग्रामरागाश्च केचन ।
इत्येष शार्ङ्गदेवस्थ संमतो मार्गवेदिनः ।।

Rama Amatya gives the date of his work as follows:

शाके नेत्रधराधराब्धिधरणीगण्येऽथ साधारणे ।
वर्षे श्रावणमासि निर्मलतरे पक्षे दशम्यां तिथौ ।।

रामामात्यविनिर्मिते स्वरतते संगीतरत्नकरात् ।
सोऽयं मेलकलानिधिर्मतिमतामाकल्पमाकल्पताम् ।।

The date of the book appears to be Shravana Shuddha 10th, Shaka year 1472, *i.e.,* A.D. 1549. I find that there is a copy of this manuscript in the Baroda Central Library. A note added by the editor of the library catalogue gives the following particulars : "Folios 2-32 dated Samvat 1628 composed by Rama Amatya, son of Todarmal Timmamatya in 1507 A.D. for Rama Raja King of Shriranga." The same editor assigns the dates A.D. 1210-1247, 15th century, A.D. 1609, to the works पारिजात, रत्नाकर, रागविबोध respectively. Personally I am of opinion that the dates of the editor are not quite reliable.

Pandit Somanatha in his *Rāga-Vibodha* says :—

द्वादश विकृतान्पूर्वे वदंति तत्र तु पृथक् पृथग्ध्वनितः ।
सप्तैव स्युर्भिन्ना न पंच यदिमे समध्वनयः ।।25।।

न पृथक् शुद्धसमाभ्यामच्युतसमकौ चतुःश्रुती च रिधौ ।
शुद्धरिधाम्यां विकृतस्त्रिश्रुतिपादपि चतुःश्रुतिपः ।।26।।

मिन्नो न चतुःश्रृतिधों निःशंकमतेऽपि कूटपुनरुक्तौ ।
तल्लक्षणतो भेदेऽप्यमीषु पंचसु न लक्ष्ये मित् ।।27।।

Somanatha gives the date of his book as follows :—

कुदहनतिथिगणितशके सौम्याद्वस्येषमासि शुचिपक्षे ।
सोमेऽग्नितिथौ रविभेऽकरोदमुं मौग्दलिः सोमः ।।

The date, therefore, appears to be the 3rd Ashvin Shuddha, Shaka year 1531, *i.e.,* A.D. 1610.

Pandit Vyankatamakhi, the author of *Chaturdandi-Prakāshikā*, in describing his *Bhupāla rāga* says :—

भूपालः प्रातरुग्देयः औडुवो मनिवर्जनात् ।
एष रागांगरागेषु गणितः शाङ्‌र्गसूरिणा ॥5-62॥

The date of the *Chaturdandi-Prakāshikā* is A.D. 1660. The late Pandit Subrahma Dikshit of Etayyapuram in Tinnevelly District told me, when I had an interview with him in 1904, that according to his information Vyankatamakhi, the author of *Chaturdandi-Prakāshikā*, was the son of Govinda Dikshit, a pupil of Tanappacharya, who carried his *guru-parampara* right up to Sharangadeva himself.

I do not think it is necessary to give any more instances to show how the Southern Sanskrit writers made attempts to connect their works with the *Ratnākara.* Even at this day, as I said, the Southerners always talk about Shārangadeva as one of their own writers. But what is it that we observe in the northern part of the country ? The name and fame of the *Ratnākara* are of course known there, but no sensible attempt seems to have been made anywhere to penetrate the mysteries of the book. None of our northern professionals seem to know what the book contains. It is only in the last century that we find one or two attempts at translating the work into the Hindi language, but the translators never seem to have understood even the *shuddha* scale of Sharangadeva and have, therefore, absolutely failed to follow his music. It would certainly be interesting to know why such a great work like the *Ratnākara* should have become absolutely unintelligible everywhere within about a hundred and fifty years of its completion. Our wonder is only increased when we see that Kallinatha,

Shārangadeva's great commentator, and the other subsequent southern writers who freely quote from his work, the *Ratnākara,* should not be in a position to explain any of the *Rāgas* described in it, notwithstanding the fact that many of these latter were such as they themselves perhaps constantly sang and played.

Some scholars have tried to explain this curious state of things by saying that Sharangadeva wrote his *Ratnākara* in the old style of *grāmas, murchhanas,* and *jātis* and thus remained unintelligible to writers in whose time the method of obtaining *Rāgas* from *Jātis* had been abolished and all music had become confined to one *grāma,* namely, the *Shadia grāma,* with its own *skuddha* and *vikrit* notes and scales. Others again say that Sharangadeva's division of music into *purvaprasiddha* and *adhunāprasiddha* leads an intelligent observer to suspect that he copied several things from some older manuscripts in his possession and in endeavouring to harmonize the music of his own time with them caused no end of confusion. His own music, they surmise, was perhaps not far removed from that of the Southern musicians. It is, no doubt unfortunate that Sharangadeva nowhere explains how the wires of his Vina were tuned and the frets adjusted thereon. If we knew that we would have at once been in a position to say what he actually sang and played. In the description which he does give of his Alapini and Kinnari Vinas, however, there appears to be some internal evidence to show that he very likely tuned their wires to Sa, Pa, Sa, Ma, just as the other Southern writers of that time did, and put about 12 or 14 frets on them. The following verses of the *Vādyādhyāya* of the *Ratnākara* might be of some interest on that point.

मुक्ततंत्रीभवं कृत्वा स्वरमाद्यं चतुर्दशम् ।
स्वरा:परे स्यु सारीणां चतुर्दशभिरंतरैः ।

सप्तकद्वयमेवं स्यादेकतारस्वराधिकम्
यथास्वं स्वरदेशांशैः श्रुतिस्तस्या विचिन्वते ।
द्वित्रास्ततोऽधिकाः सारीर्निबध्नीयात् परे त्विह ।
लक्षयंत्यंतराण्यासां स्वराविर्भावतो बुधाः ।।

My personal opinion is that until some works of the period preceding that of Shārangadeva's *Ratnakara* are found, this work is bound to defy all attempts at its solution. The only work of the pre-Ratnākara period that I have so far been able to obtain a copy of is the *"Dantila—Kohaliyam"* by Dantila and Kohala, two of Shārangadeva's predecessors. A manuscript of this name now lies in the Palace Library of Tanjore. It is a small work dealing with the art of Dancing. There is one curious circumstance in connection with this work, which is worth noting, and it is this : All the verses in this little work appear to have been faithfully incorporated in the *Nrittyādhyāya* of the *Ratnākara.* The *Dantila-Kohaliyam* is a work written by two persons and Shārangadeva in copying the verses—if at all he copied them—in his own work had, of course, to change the dual number representing the joint authorship into the singular so as to suit his own purposes. This work, however, yields no key to the music of the *Sangit Ratnākara.*

Before proceeding further, I feel it my duty to add here that some scholars have seriously taken the question of Shārangadeva's music in hand now, and it is to be hoped that their labours will be duly rewarded in the near future. *Ratnākara* is undoubtedly a very valuable link in the chain of our musical history and we shall most eagerly watch every bit of progress our learned friends make in their self-imposed and disinterested undertaking, giving them, from time to time, such humble advice and assistance as may lie in our power.

One thing, however, it will be permissible to say here and that is, that no elucidation which fails to make Sharangadeva's *rāgas* clearly intelligible, if not actually singable, will appeal to the modern music student.

Let us now turn our attention to the times of the great Emperor Akbar. I wish I could have been in a position to give you some detailed or definite information about the Gwalior School of music, which had risen into some importance before Akbar came to the throne. The School was headed by Raja Mana Singh of Gwalior himself. He is supposed to have started the modern *Dhrupad* style of singing. A *Dkrupad* is well-defined by a Sanskrit writer of the eighteenth century and I had better give the definition in his own words here for your information :—

अथ ध्रौपदलक्षणम्

गीर्वाणमध्यदेशीयभाषासाहित्यराजितम् ।
द्विचतुर्वाक्यसंपन्नं नरनारीकथाश्रयम् ॥165॥

शृंगाररसभावाढ्यं रागालापपदात्मकम् ।
पादांतानुप्रासयुक्तं पादांतयमकं च वा ॥166॥

प्रतिपादं यत्र बद्धमेवं पादचतुष्टयम् ।
उद्ग्राहध्रुवकाभोगोत्तमं ध्रुवपदं स्मृतम् ॥167॥

(*Anupa Sangita Ratnākara* by Bhavabhatta, p. 15.)

Raja Sir S. M. Tagore in his excellent compilation *"Hindu music from various authors"* at p. 213 says :—

"The Gwalior School of music dates from the time of Rajah Man Tunwar. During his reign lived the famous Nayak Bakhshu, whose melodies are only second to those of Tansen. Bakhshu also lived at the court of Raja Bikramajit, the son of Man; but when his patron lost his throne, he went to Raja

Kirat of Kalinjar. Not long afterwards he accepted a call to Gujerat where he lived at the court of Sultan Bahadur (A.D. 1526-1536). Tslemshah was also a patron of music. His two great singers were Ramdass and Mahapater. Both entered subsequently Akbar's service." (Extract from H. Blochmanns' translation of *Aini Akhari,* Vol. I.) Capt. Willard in his *"Treatise on the Music of Hindusthan"* at p. 107 says : "The most renowned of the Nayaks have been Gopal, a native of the Dekkan, who flourished during the reign of Sultan Alla-ud-din, and his contemporary Amir Khoshru of Delhi; Sultan Husain Shurquee of Jaunpur; Raja Man Quilla-dar of Gwalior and founder of the Dhrupad; Baijoo, Bhonoo, Pandvee, Bakshu, and Lohung. The four following lived at the time of Raja Man of Gwalior—Jurjoo, Bhagwan, Dhondee and Daloo." Sir W. Ouseley in his *"Anecdotes of Indian Music"* says :—"There is besides the Rāga Darpan (mirror of Rāgas) translated into Persian by Fakar Ulla from a Hindi book on the Science of music called Mankuttuhal compiled by order of Man Singh Raja of Gwalior" (Tagore's *Hindu Music from various authors,* p. 167). I had myself heard of a work called *Man Kutuhal* and believe that that is the original of Fakur Ullah's Persian work. You will be glad to learn that a copy of *Rāga Darpana* has now been secured by our noble friend and President Thakur Nawab Ali Khan (of Lucknow) and that he has consented to make a present of it to this Conference. I have great hopes that when the work is duly translated into English, it will throw a great deal of light on the condition of music in the early Mahomedan period. My friend the Thakur Saheb tells me that the book appears to contain a record, among other things, of the proceedings of a great conference of musical experts then assembled under orders from Raja Man. The book promises on that account to be very interesting indeed.

Coming then to the times of Akbar (A.D. 1556-1605) what is it that we find ? We find in fact a wonderful change in the condition of the art of Hindusthani Music. The Emperor himself was extremely fond of music and gave considerable encouragement to the cultivation of the art. I shall ask you, however, to distinguish between the cultivation of the Art and the cultivation of the study of the Science on which the Art is based. We cannot deny the force of the remark generally made that the advent in India of the Mussulman conquerors marked the date of the decline of all arts and sciences purely Hindu. The conquerors, we can easily understand, were no lovers or patrons of learning. During those unsettled times the progress of the study of the science or theory of music was bound to decline and, as a matter of fact, did decline. The practice, however, continued with more or less success until the time of Mahomed Shah, one of the successors of Aurangzeb. But we all know that theory is the real backbone of practice, and when theory perishes the practice, though it may continue to live on, is bound ultimately to drift away and run into disorder and confusion. That is exactly what seems to have happened in Northern India. The Mahomedan rulers naturally patronized at their courts their own co-religionists as musicians, who knew their tastes much better, and who by pandering to the tastes of their masters commenced to take all sorts of liberties with the orthodox Sanskrit melodies. We are told that many of the first class Hindu Pandits of those times were scared away or ceased in course of time to take the same interest in their science of music as they did formerly. I do not think anybody will be able to deny that the majority of the musicians at the court of even such a very tolerant monarch like Akbar were Mussalmans. A glance at the list of Akbar's principal musicians given in the Ain-i-Akbari will show that among the thirty-six names contained therein, there are not more than four or five which are Hindu. Now here arises a very interesting question. Did music really deteriorate by falling into the hands of the foreigners ? Personally speaking, I am not one of those who will unhesitatingly assert that the foreign contact was an unmitigated misfortune. I shall not deny that the Northern music during those times underwent some vital changes, but I am of opinion that our music gained considerably from the foreign influence. Are we not frequently told that the Southerners have more or less successfully kept the Northern contamination at arm's length, and preserved intact the ancient tradition ? Well, if their claim is true and allowable, then the condition of their music to-day should be a fairly safe index of what our own ancient music of the North really was in its pristine condition. Now, I openly ask, would you at the present moment like to throw up your current music in favour of the older one ? I do not think you would. Do not our Southern friends themselves now and then tell us from their experience that the Hindusthani music, with all its weakness in the matter of a *shastric* foundation, does possess many evident points of pleasing excellence which they would be only too glad to recommend their own professionals to carefully study and imitate ?

It was in the time of Akbar that the great Hindu Saint and musician Haridas Svami lived at Vrindavan on the banks of the sacred Jamuna. Even if we do not feel inclined to give credence to all the stories told about the miraculous effects of the Svami's music, there will be no two opinions that he was considered to be one of the greatest musicians of his time. He was Tansen's own Guru (preceptor), and that itself will be enough to silence a contrary opinion. Haridas Svami, it is said, taught eight pupils including Tansen (known as Tannamishra before his conversion to Islam), each of whom subsequently made a name for himself in India. The descendants of Tansen are now known as Seniyas. An authentic history of the descendants and representatives of Tansen is a great desideratum, in view of the accepted belief that in Akbar's time the art of Hindusthani music had reached its high water mark. The task of collecting sufficient material for such a history may not be found so difficult if we approach some of our Indian Maharajas with a request to supply us with the names of all the best artists in the employ of their States during the last two or three centuries. I should think they would be only too glad to assist us. It was again in Akbar's reign that the great poetess and musician Mirabai, wife of the Rana of Udaipur, lived. We are told that Akbar personally went and heard her. Our famous poet Tulsidas, the writer of the well-known Vishnupadas, also lived in this reign. While speaking about the musicians of Akbar's time, I think I ought to draw your attention to the works of a very eminent poet-musician by name Pundarika Vitthala, who lived and flourished about the same time. Pundarika's works must be looked upon now as simply invaluable. In the year 1907 when I was in Calcutta I happened to visit the learned oriental scholar of that city, Mahamahopadhyaya Haraprasad Shastri, M.A. That gentleman in the course of his conversation told me that he had come to read somewhere of a great Sanskrit Pandit and musician by name Parmananda Karnar, who was attached to the court of the Farqis of Khandesh about the time when Akbar ruled at Delhi. The Shastri added that, as far as he remembered, the Pandit was specially requested by the emperor to go to Delhi and write some books on the then current Hindusthani music. To the best of the Shastri's recollection Parmananda had actually written four excellent books on the subject. In the year 1908 I happened to visit the State Library of Bikaner. To my great surprise, I did not only find a name in the catalogue of the library with exactly four music works to its credit, but that name was no other than that of Pundarika Vitthala Karnataki. The four *granthas* that appeared against his name were: (1) *Sadrāgachandrodaya,* (2) *Rāgamālā,* (3) *Raga Manjari* and (4) *Nartana Nirnaya.* Suspecting that that was perhaps the Pandit whom the Mahamahopadhyaya of Calcutta meant when he mentioned the name of Parmanand Karnar, I at once applied for copies of Pundarika's works. The Library authorities granted me copies of only two of them, namely the *Sadrāgachandrodaya* and *Rāgamālā.* My surprise was greatly increased when I read the following opening verses of *Sadrāgachandrodaya*:—

वंशः फारकिभूपतेः सुसरलो भूभारधारक्षमः
श्रीमत्सग्दुणिदानिशूरविमलक्ष्मा पालशाखाबिभृत् ।
विख्यातो भुवि यत्र काव्यरसिकाः सत्कीर्तिवल्लीश्रिता-
शिचत्रं संचरतीति विश्वमखिलं के वणर्यंतीह तत् ।।२।।

तत्राभूदहमद्‌दखाननृपतिर्वीराधिवीरेश्वर-
स्त्वौदार्यादिगुणैः समस्तवसुधाधीशैः सदा राजितः ।
दृष्यच्छत्रुगणेषु च प्रविलसत्संग्रामशक्तस्तथा
संहर्ताऽविरतं दरिद्रतमसो भूमंडलाखंडलः ।।3।।

तज्जातस्ताजखानों नरपतितिलकः फारकी वै जयंतो
यंता शूरेश्वराणामरिसुभटघटाटोपजीमूतवातः।।
जातस्तातः प्रजानां भरणवितरणस्थापनाज्ञाकरेभ्यो
नित्य दानोर्मिलोलैः सकलगुणनिधी राजते राजसिंघुः ।।4।।

तज्जः श्रीबुरहानखानचतुरः कामानुकारी वरः
संगीतादिकलाप्रपूर्णविमलः साहित्यतेजोमयः ।
दारिद्यांधतमश्च यश्च गुणिनां हंताह्युदारैः करै-
र्भूमौं फारकिभूपतीशतिलकश्चंद्रश्चिरं राजते ।।5।।

(See p. 3.)

Thus I discovered that Pundarika Vitthala Pandit was really in the employ of Burhankhan, the son of Tajkhan, the son of Ahmadkhan of the Farqi dynasty. That these were rulers of Khandesh appeared from an incomplete verse as follows:—

श्रीमद्दक्षिणदिङ्युखस्य तिलके (श्रीखा) निदेशे शुभे
नित्यं भोगवतीव भोगिवसती रम्या सुपर्वादिमिः ।
अस्ति स्वस्तिकरी नरेंद्रनगरी त्वानंदवल्लीति या
तत्र श्रीबुरहानखाननृपतिः संगीतमाकर्णयत् ।।6।।

(See p. 4.)

Mr. Stanley Lane-Poole in his work *The Mahomedan Dynasties,* at p. 315, tells us the ancient history of Khandesh, where he mentions that "Akbar took Burhanpur the capital of Khandesh and received the homage of its king in A.D. 1562; but Khandesh was not fully incorporated in the Mogul Empire until 1599 A.D. when Asirgarh fell after a six months' siege." This clearly shows that Pundarika did live at the court of Burhankhan Farqi of Khandesh about the time when Akbar ruled at Delhi. It is not impossible that when Khandesh fell a victim to the forces of Akbar in A.D. 1599, Pundarika was requested to go or did go over to Delhi. There is besides, that curious coincidence too. Pundarika did actually write the four Sanskrit works I mentioned just now. At the end of the first of the four *Granthas, viz.,* the *Sadrāgachandrodaya,* Pundarika describes himself thus :—

श्रीकर्णाटजातीयपुंडरीकविठ्ठलविरचिते।
सद्रागचंद्रोदये इ.इ.

(See p. 28.)

Possibly Haraprasad Shastri mistook Parmanand Karnar for Pundarika Karnata (or Karnataki) of the South when he referred to him. That Pundarika was a great poet and a distinguished musician will readily be admitted. His Raga-Lakshanas are really most beautifully worded. It also appears that the Music of Upper India was in his time getting into confusion and his own Raja Burhankhan had ordered him to re-arrange the same. On that point Pundarika says :—

संत्यस्मिन् बहुधा विरोधगतयो लक्ष्ये च लक्ष्मोदिते
जानंतीह सुलक्ष्मपक्षविगतिं केचित्परे लौकिकीम् ।
तत्कुर्वंतु सुलक्ष्मलक्ष्यसहितं रागप्रकाशं बुधा
इत्युक्ते बुरहानखाननृपतौ बिद्वत्सभामंडले ॥7॥

(See p. 4.)

Pundarika had to undertake the very difficult task of evolving order out of chaos, and did his duty on the following excellent principle laid down by Shārangadeva, the author of the *Ratnākara,* himself.

लक्ष्यप्रधानं खलु शास्त्रमेतन्नि:शंकदेवोऽपि तदेव वष्टि।
यल्लक्ष्म लक्ष्यप्रतिबंधकं स्यात्तदन्यथा नेयमिति ब्रुवाण: ॥10॥

(See p. 4.)

As to the locality to which Pundarika's family belonged we have in the *Chandrodaya* the following information :—

कर्णाटे शैवगंगाभिधनगनिकटे सातनूर्वाव्हयों यो
ग्रामस्तत्राग्रजन्मप्रवरसुनिकराज्जामदग्न्योऽस्ति वंश: ॥
तत्र श्रीविठ्ठलार्योऽभवदमितयशास्तग्दुणाख्या तु तस्यै-
तत्सूनो रागचंद्रोदय इति च भजन् कैरवाणां मुदेऽस्तु ॥

(See p. 28.)

If we carefully examine the *rāgas* described by the poet in his *Chandrodaya* we shall not fail to observe that many of them are such as we find in the Southern books. The *shuddha* scale on which *Chandrodaya* is based is called *Mukhāri,* which corresponds with the modern *Kanakāngi* scale of the Southern musicians. In the *Rāgamālā,* Pundarika adopts the most popular and orthodox method of classifying Hindusthani melodies into *rāgas, rāginis* and *putras,* with this difference that his classification is based on most reasonable and intelligent principles. His six *rāgas* are :—

शुद्धभैरवहिंदोलो देशिकारस्तत:परम्।
श्रीराग: शुद्धनाटश्च नट्टनारायणश्च षट्।।

Both these *granthas* of Pundarika have now been published and thus there is no necessity of mentioning here the *rāginis* and *Putras* of *Rāgmālā.* The *Rāgamālā* distinctly shows that the author had come into contact with the music and musicians of North India proper, probably Delhi or Agra. The names of *rāgas* like *Chaitri, Gowdi, Musali, Irāq, Bākharej, Yemen, Husaini, Tirban,* etc., which appear in the *Rāgādhydya* will speak for themselves. I am inclined to think, that Pundarika wrote his *Rāgamālā* after he arrived in the north with or without the orders of the Emperor. We shall have to take particular notice of this poet's works because we have here an instance of an admittedly Southern Pandit being asked to systematize the music of Northern India. It is interesting to observe that the Pandit while adopting a different terminology for his *Rāgamālā,* most cleverly manages to keep in touch with the system in which he was born. He describes his *shuddha* and *vikrit svaras* thus :—

षड्जादीनां स्थिति: प्रोक्ता प्रथमा भरतादिभि: ।
असपा: पूर्वपूर्वास्ते संचरंत्युत्तरोत्तरम् ।
त्रिस्त्रिगंतीस्ते प्रत्येकं याति गश्च चतुर्गती: ।
यद्यद्रागोपयोग: स्यात्तत्तदिच्छागतिर्भवेत् ।।
गन्योर्गती द्वितीये चांतरकाकलिनौ स्मृतौ ।।

A careful observer will find from the *granthas* of Pundarika that the latter does not use more than fourteen *svara*—names in describing his ragas. The *Vinąprakarana* will also show that the author tuned the wires of his *vinā* to the *svaras* सा प सा म and put only twelve frets on the keyboard thereof. All the Southern writers have always done the same, and I believe that is the practice even this day throughout the whole country. In the time of Pundarika all music was sung and played to one *grāma* only, namely the *shadja-grdma.*

Akbar died in the year A.D. 1605. He was succeeded by his son Jehangir who ruled at Delhi from A.D. 1605 to 1627. We do not know definitely how many of Akbar's musicians he continued in his service, but probably several of them had gone away. The Tuzuk and the Iqbalnamah mention the following singers of Jehangir's reign : Jehangirdad, Chatar-khan, Parwizdad, Khurramdad, Makhu and Hamzan. Tulsidas, the popular poet, died in this reign.

The popular Sanskrit work *Sangita Darpana* written by Pandit Damodara, the son of Lakshmidhara, is supposed to have been composed about the year A.D. 1625, and if this date be correct, it will follow that the same must have been written when Jehangir was on the throne of Delhi. We have at present nothing like reliable evidence to state where Pandit Damodara lived and flourished. That *Sangita Darpana* was translated into Persian long before the latter half of the 18th century A.D., appears from a reference to the book in the essay *The musical modes of the Hindus,* written by that great Orientalist Sir William Jones. There the learned scholar says :—

"Let us proceed to the Indian system which is minutely explained in a great number of Sanskrit books by authors who leave arithmetic and geometry to the astronomers and properly discourse on music as an art confined to the pleasures of imagination. The Pandits of this province (Bengal) unanimously prefer the *Damodara* to any of the popular Sangitas; but I have not been able to procure a good copy of it and am perfectly satisfied with the *Narayan* which I received from Benares, and in which the *Damodara* is frequently quoted. The Persian book (Toft-ul-Hind) "a present from India" was composed under the patronage of Aazem Shah by the very diligent and ingenious Mirzakhan, and contains a minute account of Hindu literature in all or most of its branches; he professes to have extracted his elaborate chapter on music with the assistance of pandits from the *Rāgārnava* (Sea of passion), the *Rāga Darpana,* (the mirror of modes), and *Sabhāvinoda* (Delight of Assemblies) and some other approved treatises in Sanskrit. The *Sangit Darpana* which he also names among his authorities has been translated into Persian." Damodara Pandit in his *Rāgādhyāya* cites Kallinatha's opinion as his authority in one place, which will clearly show that his *Sangit Darpana* must have been written after the first half of the fifteenth century. Whatever the merits or popularity of *Darpana* may have been in Northern India in the seventh century, it has to be confessed that the work has become at the present day as unintelligible and mysterious as the *Sangita-Ratnākara* of Sharangadeva from which Damodara freely copies the whole of his material for *Svarādhyāya.* I shall not be far wrong if I say that we in the west of India do not treat the work with any very great respect. But, for such a state of things Pandit Damodara has himself to thank. He adopts in his work the *svarādhyāya* of Sharangadeva and tacks on to it the *rāgadhyāya* of some other unknown author without assigning any the least reason or explanation for such an unusual and unnatural procedure. I am aware, some of our ignorant professionals take particular care to learn by heart the different pictorial descriptions of *rāgas* given in the book, but I am quite certain that they know nothing about the real significance or secret of those descriptions. It is, however, not necessary for us here to criticize either *Sangit Darpana* or its author Damodara Pandit and we shall proceed to our next point.

Jehangir died in A.D. 1627. His son Shahjahan succeeded him. While considering the history of music in the time of this Emperor (1627-1658 A.D.) it will be most convenient to take notice of that most popular Sanskrit work of Northern India which is known as *Sangita-Pārijāta.* It was written by Pandit Ahobala the son of Shrikrishna. The exact date of the book cannot be ascertained but some scholars are of opinion that it was written about 230 years ago. Sir Ouseley in his *Oriental Collections,* Vol. I, tells us that *Sangita Pārijāta* was translated into Persian by Dinanatha, the son of Basudeo, in the year A.D. 1724. *Pārijāta* has also been quoted by Pandit Bhavabhatta who lived and flourished about 200 years ago. I do not propose to trouble you with a full description of the *svara* and *rāga* systems of Ahobala, as most of you are, no doubt, quite familiar with them. My own opinion is that Ahobala Pandit has access to the *Rāga Tarangini* of Lochanakavi and also to *Rāga Vibodha* of the Southern writer Somanatha. The *shuddka* scale of *Sangita Pārijāta* is the same as that of *Tarangini.* Ahobala lays down 29 *vikrita-svara* names, but when he comes to describe his *rāgas* he drops many of them, as will appear from the following *shlokas* which appear at the end of the *Rāgadhyāya* of *Pārijdta* :—

पूर्वकोमलतीवैश्च तथा तीव्रतरेण च
अतितीव्रतमेनैव सर्वे रागा उदीरिताः।
रिंच पूर्व तथा तीव्रं तीव्रतरं च गस्वरम्

तीव्रतमं तया गं च मं च तीव्रस्वरं तथा ॥
गंच तीव्रतमं धंच पूर्वास्यं तीवसंज्ञितम् ।
तीव्रतरं निषादं च तीव्रतमं च निस्वरम् ॥
इत्येतांश्च दश त्यक्त्वा रागलक्षणभीरितम् ॥
द्वादशभिर्विकाराधैः शुद्धैश्च सप्तमिः स्वरैः ।
एतैः कृत्वा प्रसिद्धा ये त एवात्र प्रकीर्तिताः ॥

(Verses 493-497.)

In my opinion these verses are really very important because they throw a good deal of light on the question, how many *svaras* were actually used by Ahobala Pandit in his *Ragalakshanas*. The *shlokas* would at first sight lead the reader to conclude that the Pandit made use of 19 *svaras* in his descriptions of the *rāgas,* but as a matter of fact he did not do so. These verses are to be taken subject to the explanation given in the following stanzas :

ऋषभः शुद्ध एवासौ पूर्वगांधार ईष्यते ।
गांधारः शुद्धएवासौ रिस्तीव्रतर ईष्यते ॥
अतितीव्रतमो गः स्यान्मध्यमः शुद्ध एव हि ।
धैवतः शुद्ध एवासौ निषादः पूर्वसंज्ञकः ॥
निषादः शुद्ध एवासौ धस्तीव्रतर ईष्यते ।
एवं स्यात् सर्वयंत्रेषु स्वरस्थानस्य लक्षणम् ॥

(Verses 324-326.)

The practice of calling the same *svara* by two or more different names was, as you know, quite common in those days. These three verses will practically reduce the number of *vikrits* to seven only and when you go further and remove the *svara* names कोमल ग and कोमल नी which Ahobala nowhere uses in his *ragas,* we find that the Pandit never used more than 12 notes in singing or playing his 122 *rdgas* described in the *Pārijāta.*

There is another point on which Ahobala puts the whole musical world of India under his obligation and it is this. He was the first musician who distinctly saw the absolute necessity of describing his 12 *svaras* in terms of the lengths of the speaking wire of the Vina. I need hardly dwell upon that part of the subject here because the question of Ahobala's *svaras* has been fully treated in articles which have appeared just recently in certain journals and magazines. I said just a moment ago, that Ahobala had very likely access to Somanatha's *Rāga Vibodha* and shall now give the reasons which induce me to draw that inference. Somanatha Pandit in his *Raga Vibodha,* unlike the writers of his time, makes use of the *svara* names मृदुसा, मृदुम, and मृदुप to denote the sounds of the third *Shruti* of each of the notes सा, म and प. Ahobala in his *Parijāta* refers to these notes as follows :—

तथा तीव्रतमो गोऽपि मृदुर्ग इति कीर्तितः।।
मश्च तीव्रतमोऽप्युक्तो मृदुर्म इति पंडितैः।।

Rāga Vibodha was written in the Shaka year 1531, *i.e.* A.D. 1610. The author, as I said, gives the date of his work in the following *Arya* :—

कुदहनतिथिगणितशके सौम्याब्दस्येषमासि शुचिपक्षे।
सोमेऽग्रितिथौ रविभेऽकरोदमुं मौग्दलिः सोमः।।

It will be useful to say a few words about this *Grantha Rāga Vibodha* here, although as I have already told you Somanatha is now admitted to be a Southern writer. I wish to refer to his work here only because it clearly shows that the author had himself come under the influence of the music of Northern India. He uses in the *Rāga Vibodha* the *svara*- names of both the Southern and the Northern systems of music. It is impossible to say whether he had obtained a copy of the *Rāga Tarangini* also, because the only names of his predecessors he refers to in his book are हनुमान्, मतंग, निःशंक, and कल्लनाथ. His use of the *svara* names तीव्र तीव्रतर, तीव्रतम, and of the term *"Thāta"* as a synonym for *"Meta,"* will also show that he had come into contact with Northern music. He does not, however, appear to have lived for a sufficiently long time in the North, because a careful perusal of his *Svarādhyāya* shows that he misunderstood some of the Upper India technicalities. The way in which he places his 12 frets on the Veena again does not appear to be quite satisfactory. Many scholars are now inclined to suspect that it was Somanatha's *Rāga Vibodha* that was responsible to a certain extent for the perplexity into which Ahobala found himself when he made his attempt to reconcile his own terminology with that of the Southern writers. Nobody will, however, deny that both these writers were great Sanskrit scholars and, we shall presume, great musicians too. Their works may safely be cited as instances of the tendency of those times to establish good musical relations between the North and the South. The importance of *Sangita Pārijāta* again, I believe, can never be exaggerated. It is one of our great landmarks in the history of Northern Music. The *Shuddha* scale of *Sangita Pārijāta* is the same as that of our modern *Kāphi Rāga.* This scale will correspond with the southern scale *Kharaharapriya.* It will be interesting one of these days, to determine where Somanatha himself obtained this *svara* name मृदुपंचम from. He had a copy of Sharangadeva's *Ratnākara* before him and it is possible he took the same from the definition of the third variety of *Saindhavi*—given in that book. *Saindhavi* is there defined thus :—

मालवे कैशिकेप्यस्ति सैंधवी मृदुपंचमा।।
समंद्रा निगमैर्युक्ता षड्जन्यासग्रहांशिका।
प्रयोज्या सर्वभावेषु श्रीसोढलसुतोदिता।।182।।

(*Rāgadhyaya,* Part II.)
(p. 223 *Ratnākara.)*

The principal musicians at the court of Shah Jehan according to the Ain-i-Akbari were Jagannatha who received from the Emperor the title ot Kaviraja; Dirang Khan; and Lal Khan who got the title of Gunasamudra (Ocean of excellence). Lal Khan was a son-in-law of Bilas Khan a son of Tansen. We are told Jagannatha and Dirang Khan were both weighed in silver and received Rs 4,500 each. Shah Jehan died in A.D. 1658, and after a short quarrel among his sons for the throne Aurangzeb succeeded him. Aurangzeb tried to abolish every trace of music from his court. Stanley Lane-Poole in his life of Aurangzeb, (Rulers of India series, p. 101) says :—"Aurangzeb did his best to suppress music and dancing altogether in accordance with the example of the Mahomedan Prophet, who was born without an ear for music and therefore hastily ascribed the invention of harmony to the Devil. The musicians of India were certainly noted for a manner of life which ill accorded with Aurangzeb's strict ideas and their concerts were not celebrated for sobriety. The Emperor determined to destroy them and a severe edict was issued. Raids of the police dissipated their harmonious meetings and their instruments were burnt. One Friday as Aurangzeb was going to the mosque he saw an immense crowd of singers following a bier and rending the air with their cries and lamentations. They seemed to be burying some great prince. The Emperor sent to inquire the cause of the demonstration and was told it was the funeral of music slain by his orders and wept by her children. 'I approve their piety,' said Aurangzeb, 'let her be buried deep and never be heard again.' Of course the concerts went on in the palaces of the nobles but they never were heard at court. The Emperor seriously endeavoured to convince the musicians of the error of their ways and those who reformed were honoured with pensions." We need not, therefore, pause to say anything more about the music of Aurangzeb's time.

The next Pandit whose works will deserve special notice will be Bhavabhatta who, according to his own *Granthas,* was attached to the court of a Raja by name Anupasinha. Bhavabhatta gives his own pedigree in his *Anupasangita Ratnākara* thus :—

कृष्णात्रगोत्रसंभूतं कुलमांभीरदेशजं ।
पुर धवलमित्याहुः प्रपिता तानभट्टकः ।।
पिता जनार्दनः साक्षाज्जनार्दन इवापरः ।
मातुःस्वप्रभवे नाम भावेत्युक्तं स्वपूर्वजैः।।

At the end of the *Rāgadhyāya of* his work *Anupankusha* he says :—

इतिश्रीमद्राठोडकुलदिनकरमहाराजाधि
राजश्रीकर्णसिंहात्मजजयश्री विराजमान-
चतुःसमुद्रमुद्रावच्छिन्नमेदिनीप्रतिपालन
चतुरवदान्यातातिशयनिर्जितचिंतामणिस्व-
प्रतापतापितारिवर्गधर्मावतारश्रीमहारा-
जाधिराजश्रीमदनूपसिंहप्रमोदितश्रीमहीम-
हेंद्रमौलिमुकुटरत्नकिरणनीराजितचरण-
कमलश्रीसाहिजहांसभामंडलमंडनसंगीतराजज-
नादंनभट्टांगजानुष्टुप्चक्रवर्तिसंगीतराजभा-
वभट्टविरचितः श्रीसंगीतानुपांकुश ग्रंथः समाप्तः ।।

From these quotations we learn that Bhavabhatta's father's name was Janardanabhatta and that he lived and flourished at the court of Emperor Shah Jehan. He had obtained from the Emperor, it appears, the title or "Sangit Raja." Bhavabhatta's ancestors belonged to Dhavalpur in the province of Abhira (Eastern Rajputana and Malwa). Bhavabhatta himself was in the employ of Raja Anupasinha, the son of Karanasinha, and seems to have obtained some titles like संगीतराज अनुष्टुपचक्रवर्ती. Here now there will be a very interesting question to consider. Could the music expert Jagannatha of Shah Jehan, who had obtained the title Kaviraja from the Emperor, be the same as Bhavabhatta's own father and no one else ? Possibly he was. The period following the death of Shah Jehan, we know, was most unfavourable for the cultivation of music and it is quite probable, Janardanabhatta or his son Bhavabhatta came over to Bikaner and entered the service of Anupasinha. History tells us that some of the Rajputana chiefs were very powerful in those days and gave refuge to many pandits and artists who were scared away from the court of Aurangzeb. Bhavabhatta appears to have been a good Sanskrit scholar and also a well-known musician. His family seems to have originally belonged to some ancient southern stock, although later on some of his ancestors came and settled in the north. The Pandit refers to the following authorities in his work *Anupasangita Ratnākara*:—

1. Sangit Ratnākara.
2. Sangit Darpana.
3. Svarmelakalānidhi.
4. Rāga Vibodha.
5. Sangit Kalpavriksha.
6. Rāgatatva Vibodha.

7. Rāga Kautuka.
8. Sangitopanishada.
9. Nrityanirnaya.
10. Sadrāgachandrodaya.
11. Rāga Manjari.
12. Sangit Pārijāta.
13. Hridayaprakāsha.
14. Rāga Mālā.

All these works are even now available in the Palace Library of Bikaner. A careful examination of Bhavabhatta's own *Granthas, Anupasangita Ratnākara, Anupa Vilās* and *Anupānkusha,* will show that he too had failed to follow clearly the music of Shārangadeva's Ratnākara. He merely quotes *Ratnākara sklokas* here and there and leaves his readers to follow them as best they can. I think I have already said that that has been the way all old Sanskrit writers in the country have used *Ratnākara.* Not a single *Rāga* of *Ratnākara* has been successfully handled by any writer, although almost every author has spoken of the work with the greatest respect. The *shuddha* scale on which Bhavabhatta bases his system is *Mukhari.* In his *Anupasangita Ratnākara* he classifies all his *Rāgas* under the following twenty *Melas* or *Thatas* :—

1. Todi.
2. Goudi.
3. Varāti.
4. Kedāra.
5. Shuddha Nāta.
6. Mālavakaishika.
7. Shri.

8. Hamira.
9. Ahiri.
10. Kalyāna.
11. Deshākshi.
12. Deshakāra.
13. Sāranga.
14. Karnāta.
15. Kāmoda.
16. Hizāja.
17. Nadarāmakri.
18. Hindola.
19. Mukhāri.
20. Soma.

His *Mukhāri* scale is the same as the present *Shuddha* scale of the southern musicians. Bhāvabhatta's works will be very interesting to our modern music scholars, because many of his *Rāgalakshanas* will even now be useful to them. I do not propose, however, to take the Conference through them as it is not necessary to do so. The classification of his *Rāgas* by Bhāvabhatta and the *Shuddha* scale on which he founds it will be enough evidence to draw the inference that he came originally from some ancient southern stock. His works will be of great interest to us also because we find in them another attempt to re-arrange and systematize the drifting music of Northern India. The manner in which the Pandit adopts the northern *Lakshanas* of *Rāgas* and applies to them the Shastric method of the southern writers is really very clever.

We all know that the chief characteristic of the southern *Shuddha* scale lies in the fact that the *Vikritis* of *Shuddha Svaras* are only their higher pitches. In the *Tarangini* and

Pārijāta, which are looked upon as genuine Northern *Granthas,* the position of the *Shuddha Svara* is the central one. When the *Shuddha Svara* is lowered it becomes कोमल or flat, to use the northern technical language, and when it is raised it is said to become तीव्र or sharp. I think I had better illustrate my meaning by one or two concrete examples. You are aware that our Hindusthani *Bhairavi Rāga* is called *Todi* by the musicians of the Southern presidency. Bhavabhatta Pandit describes his *Todi Thata* as follows:—

तोडीमेलः प्रसिद्धः स्यादेकैकगतिकौ निगौ।
मेलादतस्तोडिकाद्याः कतिचित्तु भवंति हि।।

(Anupa Sangita Ratnākara 187.)

Here, by his एकैकगतिकौनिगौ he merely means the *komala Ga,* and *Komala Ni,* of the Hindusthani musicians and the *sadhārana Ga,* and *kaishika Ni,* of the southern musicians. His *Gowdi Thāta* again is the Hindusthani *Bhairava Thāta.* He defines it thus:— निगौ तृतीयगतिकौ गौडिमेलः प्रकीर्तितः The तृतियगतिक नि and ग, may be taken as the Hindusthani *tivra Ga* and *tivra Ni,* and the southern *antara Ga* and *kakali Ni.* His *shuddha Ri* and *shuddha Dha* were, of course, the same as those of the southern musicians, and corresponded with the Hindusthani *komala Ri* and *komala Dha.*

It will be very interesting to compare the terminology of Bhavabhatta with that of Pundarika Vitthala. In the *Sadrāga Chandrodaya* the तृतियगतिक ग and तृतियगतिक नि of Bhavabhatta will correspond with लघु मध्यम and लघु षड्ज respectively. In his *Rāgamālā* Pundarika uses the same names for these notes as Bhavabhatta does, *viz.,* तृतियगतिक ग and तृतियगतिक नि.

Before leaving Bhavabhatta and coming to more modern times, I wish to mention to you another Sanskrit work of some importance. It is the *"Hridayaprakāsha"* by one Hridyanārāyandeva. I have not yet been able to obtain a copy of it, but I have seen some quotations from it in Bhavabhatta's works. It appears to be a purely northern authority with a *Shuddha* scale like that of the *Rāga Tarangini.* I am told the book is available in the Bikaner State Library.

The death of Aurangzeb (A.D. 1707) brings us to the beginning of the eighteenth century. There were ten successors of Aurangzeb who ruled at Delhi between A.D. 1707 and 1857. During that period music did continue to be cultivated but not with the vigour it had attained in the preceding reigns. In the latter half of the eighteenth century the Mahomedan power commenced to decline and the country began to come under the influence of our present rulers. Raja Sir S. M. Tagore, in his *"Universal History of Music"* p. 58 says as follows :— "Mahomed Shah (A.D. 1719) was the last of the Emperors who had renowned musicians at his court. There are many vocal compositions extant which are associated with his name." The well-known singers and composers Adāranga and Sadāranga flourished at the court of this emperor. "The famous Shori brought the *Tappā* style of singing to its highest degree of perfection. The chief feature of music of the Mahomedan period was the beautiful combination of Hindu style with the Persian one. Some types of classical music were under the Persian names while some entirely new ones were introduced, such as *Trivata, Taranā, Guzal, Rekhtā, Quāl, Kulbānāh,* etc. The style of music the Mahomedans cultivated is now supposed to be the standard high class music of India, leaving out, of course, the provincial airs." Capt. Willard who published the *"Treatise on the music of Hindusthan"* in the first half of the nineteenth century tells us about the musicians of the closing days of the Mahomedan period as follows :—

"In more modern times Sadarang and Udharang, Noorkhan, Ladkhan, Pyarkhan, Janee and Gulam Rusool, Shukkur and Mukhun, Tethoo and Meethoo, Mahomed Khan and Chhujookhan and Shoree the founder of the *Tuppa,* stand in high repute; and several practical musicians of both sexes are even now to be met with, who although ignorant of the theory of music, may for extent, sweetness, pliability and perfect command of the voice, rival some of the first rate minstrels of Europe. Mahomed Khan and Serho Baee amongst others whom I have heard are living examples of superior vocal powers; and Khooshal Khan and Oomraokhan, *Bin* players, of instrumental execution. Good performers of other instruments are more numerous."

In the early British period, music came to be more or less confined to the courts of the leading native princes. The Europeans, as a general rule, looked upon it as semi-barbarous. I am aware, several Oriental scholars like Sir William Jones, Dr. Griffiths and others made some attempts to study the subject, but the records they have left go to show that their interest in it was not more than academic or antiquarian. Under the British rule Indian music did not get any special patronage from Government, for obvious reasons, and the necessary consequence was that it commenced to deteriorate both in quality and quantity. Until about two or three decades ago the Hindusthani music had fallen into the most deplorable neglect. Even the native princes who in olden times showed a great deal of favour and sympathy towards it, under the new system of education they received, began to be entirely indifferent to it. The result was that the older race of musicians died away without leaving their best art to their descendants and representatives. I am afraid that is one of the reasons why we now find so few first-class artists in the country. I am prepared to admit that some experts of the front rank are even now to be found in some of our native courts, but I shall not hesitate to say that their number is exceedingly small.

I shall proceed to notice some of the leading authorities of the last century now. About the *Fasli* year 1224, corresponding with A.D. 1813, one Mahomed Rezza (a nobleman of Patna according to Raja Sir S. M. Tagore) wrote his work called *Nagmāt-e-Āsaphi.* Rezba seems to have been thoroughly dissatisfied with the absurd and meaningless *Rāga-Rāgini —Putra* classifications of his time, and took it into his head to introduce some sort of intelligent principle in them. He boldly criticized all the four *Matas* (*viz., Bharata mata, Hanumāna mata, Kallinātha mata* and *Someshvara mata)* wrongly respected in his time, and pronounced them as entirely out-of-date and unsuited to the spirit and practice of the times, and then laid down his own *mata* as follows:—

राग नाम	**रागिनी नाम**
1. भैरव:	(i) भैरवी, (ii) रामकली, (iii) गुजरी, (iv) खट, (v) गांधारी, (vi) आसावरी
2. मालकौंस:	(i) वागेश्वरी, (ii) तोडी, (iii) देशी, (iv) सुहा, (v) सुध राई, (vi) मुलतानी।
3. हिंडोल:	(i) पुरिया, (ii) वसंत, (iii) ललत, (iv) पंचम, (v) धनाश्री, (vi) मारवा।
4. श्री	(i) गौरी, (ii) पूर्वी, (iii) गौरा, (iv) त्रिवण, (v) मालश्री, (vi) जेताश्री।
5. मेघ	(i) मधुमाध, (ii) गौंड, (iii) शुद्धसारंग, (iv) बडहंस, (v) सामंत, (vi) सोरट।
6. नट	(i) छायानाट, (ii) हमीर, (iii) कल्याण, (iv) केदार, (v) बिहागडा, (vi) यमन।

The great principle which he clearly enunciated for *Rāga-Rāgini* classifications was that there should be some similarity or common features between the *rāga* and its *rāginis*. Nobody will deny that his own classification does show that he acted up to his principle. Rezza was no doubt a talented musician. I wish we had men of his type now. I shall here draw your attention to one or two points in connection with this work which will be of some historical importance to us.

In the *Nagmāt-e-Āsaphi,* for the first time, do we come across a reliable authority with the *Bilāval* scale for its *Shuddha* scale. This scale, as you know, is the foundation scale of our modern Hindusthani music. It corresponds, as I have already said, very nearly with the European scale of C major. I say "very nearly" advisedly because the sixth note of our Hindusthani *Shuddha scale* is slightly higher than that of the European scale. I have also remarked that it would be a matter of the greatest importance to our music historians to find out when and how the *Bilāval* scale came to supplant the older *Shuddha* scales of Upper India. *Nagmāt* was written, it appears, in the time of Asaf-ud-dawla, the Nawab of Ajodhya. The author tells us that he wrote the book after fully consulting all the available best artists of the day, probably in a conference under the presidentship of the Nawab. Many of the *rāga* definitions of *Nagmāt* will be found useful even at this day by our Hindusthani musicians. Our worthy president has fortunately procured a copy of the work, and you will be glad to learn that he is going to present the same to the Conference.

While these things were happening in the northern part of the country, curiously enough, a similar movement had been set on foot in Western India. Maharaja Pratap Singh Deva of Jaipur, who ruled in that city from A.D. 1779 to 1804, took it into his head to call his own Pandits and experts together and in consultation with them made an attempt to get a standard work on Hindusthani music written. He named it *"Sangita Sāra."* It is not necessary to go into a detailed survey of that work on this occasion, but I may observe here that the literary talent available to the Maharaja at that time does not appear to have been of a very superior order. The work refers to good many Sanskrit authorities, notably *Ratnākara, Darpana, Rāgamālā, Anupa Vilas, Pārijāta* and others, but the Pandits of Maharaja Pratap Singh do not seem to have followed or rightly understood even one of them ! I do not deny, however, that the work has its own value all the same. The *Rdga Lakshanas* as coming from the great professional artists of the Raja's court will certainly give us some valuable assistance in judging the correctness or otherwise of those in use now. But here I ought to warn you that music has always been a progressive art and the great principle which should guide us in judging the correctness or value of current practice is the one which Sharangadeva Pandit himself has laid down; *viz.* :—

अथवा लक्ष्यप्रधानानि शास्त्राण्येतानि मन्वते।
तस्माल्लक्ष्यविरुद्धं यच्छास्त्रं नेयं तदन्यथा।।

The *Tālādhyāya, Vādyādhyāya,* and *Nrityādhyāya* of *Sangit Sāra* will certainly repay the reader's labour. We shall never hesitate to give the work its own value in our historical survey of the music of Northern India. It was a praiseworthy attempt on the part of the Maharaja to preserve in writing the opinions of the best available experts of the period. The *Shuddha* scale of *Sangit Sāra* appears to be Bilāval, a fact which is worth taking note of.

The next important *Grantha* of the nineteenth century that will have to be noticed is the *Sangita Rāgakalpadruma* of Krishnananda Vyas. The author describes himself as follows:—

देवीं वाक्पतिमीश्वरं गणपति नत्वा हरिं मारुतिं।।
संगीतं भरतेशमारुतिमतं सम्यग्विचार्यादरात्।।
इंद्रप्रस्थसमुभ्दवं विरचित यत्तानसेनादिभि-।
स्तद्वयक्त प्रकरोति नादनिलंय श्रीरागकल्पद्रुमम्।।
पौत्रोऽहममरानन्द वेदव्यासद्विजन्मनः।
पुत्रश्च हीरकानन्द वेदव्यासस्य धीमतः।।
कृष्णानन्दाभिधो वेदव्यासो नत्वा सरस्वतीं।
रागकल्पद्रुमं नाम कुर्वे ग्रंथं सतां मुदे।।

The book was published at Calcutta in May 1842. I have the greatest admiration for the industry and patience of the author who could bring into existence a gigantic compilation of those proportions. There is not much to be said in favour of the Sanskrit *Shastric* lore contained in the few opening pages of the book. There Mr. Vyas simply puts together the *Svara* and *Rāga Adhyāyas* of *Ratnākara, Darpana, Rāgamdlā,* and one or two other minor works, and then proceeds to his chief work of collecting together all the available masterpieces in existence of Hindi composition that he could lay his hands on. As the author gives only the wording of the compositions without notation, his collection fails to help the practical singer, although as a record of the original wordings, the same will be found very useful. The *Shuddha* scale of Krishnanand Vyas appears to be also Bilavala.

In the latter half of the last century will come the monumental work of that great musician and scholar of Bengal, Raja Sir S. M. Tagore, whose achievements in and services to our national music would scarcely be surpassed for many years to come. The Raja's publications are too numerous to mention here. Bengal is rightly proud of him. Some of the publications like *Kanthakaumudi, Sangita Sāra,* and *Yantrakshetradipikā* will speak for themselves. There is another work in Bengali, named *Gita Sutra Sāra,* written by my friend the late Mr. Krishna Dhan Banerji of Cooch Behar, which also deserves special mention. Mr. Banerji has written in that book about a hundred *Dhrupads* and *Khyals* to European Notation in a very clever manner.

Of the vernacular publications of the last two or three decades I do not propose to say anything because a discussion of their merits and short-comings here would unnecessarily involve invidious comparisons and arouse hostile feelings. Their number besides is too large to admit of an impartial and just review. They have in their own way done important and useful service. They have aroused our educated classes from their attitude of apathy towards music and created in them a desire to learn and cultivate the art. I should say this in itself is no small achievement. There is one thing, however, which an intelligent observer misses in many of our recent publications. The writers of the majority of these books do not seem to show a very clear grasp of the great system lying at the foundation of the Hindusthani music as it is now sung. It is not my purpose to expatiate here to-day on the merits of a system. You all know that in the absence of a systematic method of musical instruction there is but very little chance of making satisfactory progress. Merely writing a few disconnected songs to a self-invented notation, even with a few remarks here and there as to the differentiating characters of the *Ragas* employed therein will not, in my opinion, supply the place or want of a real music system. It will be necessary to go further and fully explain the main principles on which the whole system in based as also to show in a perfectly intelligent manner how the *Rāgas* are interconnected, and take their respective parts in the general plan or design. It is this that we miss in the majority of the recent publications. Some of these writers seem to forget again the most important point that in these modern times everything that is written or said must be perfectly clear and candid and the same must also appeal to the commonsense, reason and intelligence of the reader or listener, if the latter is intended to take a genuine interest in the statement. You will all agree that the reading public will always appreciate writings which will really illumine and not dazzle.

Having said so much about the history of our music during the last six centuries we shall now briefly recapitulate the most important points of the historical survey we have taken of the Hindusthani music. Thus, you saw :—

(a) That none of the old Sanskrit writers whose works, we considered, used the Bilāval scale as their *Shuddha* scale.

(b) That almost all the Sanskrit and vernacular writers on music have actually used twelve (rarely fourteen) notes to the scale in describing their *Rāgas,* and have put only twelve frets on the *Veenā.*

(c) That the *Rāgas* of our old writers, as a general rule, were distinguished from each other by their *Ārohas, Āvarohas* and *Vādi* notes.

(d) That during the last five centuries at least all music in the country seems to have been confined to the *Shadja Grāma* alone.

(e) That the confinement of music to one *Grāma (viz., Shadja Grāma)* introduced such important changes in the old musical scale that the method of obtaining

Rāgas from the *Jātis* (as propounded by Pandit Sharangadeva and some others) had to be abolished; but the abolition had the most desirable effect of ultimately setting free vocal music from the domination of instrumental music.

(f) That it appears that the southern Pandits now and then came to the northern parts of the country with a view to study the *Rāga* systems prevailing there and *vice versa.*

(g) That ever since the time of the advent of the Mahomedans into the country the music of Northern India has been losing its touch with the ancient Sanskrit *Shastras* and has been systematically gathering foreign elements.

(h) That at long intervals attempts appear to have been made to collect, rearrange, assimilate, and consolidate existing practices so as to reduce the same to some intelligible and easily workable system.

(i) That even the Southern Pandits would appear to have taken part in the work of such systematization with the approval of the then ruling kings and princes.

(j) That the last great attempt in that direction seems to have been made in the beginning of the last century.

(k) That there seems to have been no attempt made, as far as we could see, to write a systematic treatise in Sanskrit on the modern Hindusthani music during the last hundred years.

(l) That a student of Hindusthani music in these days will have to consider the following music works as his great landmarks :—

(1) *Rāga Tarangini* by Lochan Kavi.

(2) *Sadrāga Chandrodaya* by Pundarika Vitthala.
(3) *Rāga Manjari* by Pundarika Vitthala.
(4) *Rāga Mālā* by Pundarika Vitthala.
(5) *Nartana Nirnaya* by Pundarika Vitthala.
(6) *Anupa Ratnākara* by Pandit Bhavabhatta.
(7) *Anupa Vilāsa* by Pandit Bhavabhatta.
(8) *Anupānkusha* by Pandit Bhavabhatta.
(9) *Hridayaprakāsh* by Hridayanarayandeva.
(10) *Nagmāt-e-Āsaphi* by Mahomed Rezza.
(11) *Sangita Sāra* by Maharaja Pratap Singh.
(12) *Sangita Kalpadruma* by Krishnananda Vyas.

The question before us now will be, how do we stand from the point of view of music ? The answer to the question is very simple and it is in fact this. We find to-day that the standard high class music of Northern India is no other than that which the Mahomedan professional artists have introduced during the last five centuries or so. Our old Sanskrit *Granthas,* even such as are available to us now, are scarcely looked upon as binding authorities because the practical music in use now contravenes their directions on some of the most important points. Our *Granthas* having thus become inapplicable to the current practice, we naturally have come to be thrown on the mercy of our illiterate, ignorant, and narrow-minded professionals. Our modern scholars have distinctly seen the disadvantages of this unsatisfactory state of things but in the absence of proper helps and facilities they find themselves unable to control the situation just at present. There is no lack of excellent material in our Hindusthani music for the reconstruction of a good workable music system. The following general features, for instance, of our Hindusthani music, will easily suggest to an intelligent observer the means of evolving an excellent *Shāstric* foundation for a good music system :—

(1) During the last three or four hundred years, the various treatises systematizing the music of the country seem to have been written on the basis of the twelve notes of the scale so commonly known.

(2) All our writers on music, whether ancient or modern, seem to accept the principle of laying down the parent modes or *Thātas* first and then classifying the *Rāgas* under them.

(3) There seems to be a perfect agreement as to the division of *Rāgas* into the three main classes, (1) *Odava,* (2) *Shādava,* and (3) *Sampurna.*

(4) As a general rule, a *Rāga* to be legitimate is bound to have at least five of the twelve notes of the scale.

(5) No Rāga is allowed to drop *Ma* and *Pa* notes at the same time.

(6) And, as a general rule, a *Rāga* is not allowed to use two notes of the same denomination consecutively except in a very few special cases.

It is not necessary to enumerate any more of such features, as this will be enough to make my meaning clear. Fortunately for us the Southern music system also, recognizes almost all these important rules and that will save us the trouble of inventing an entirely new *Shāstric* basis for our system. We can, without sacrificing anything of our own Northern system, safely adopt the basic principles of such of the Southern authorities as will suit us and erect a magnificent music structure thereon, for the use of our own music-loving public. Here I wish not to be misunderstood. I know, as well as you do, that our Hindusthani system is perfectly independent of the Southern or Karnatik system. Personally I am a lover and a devotee of the Northern system, which I have studied under Northern masters, but I may frankly tell you that my sentiments towards the other system are anything but antipathetical. I honestly believe that time has now arrived when there ought to be a fair exchange of good points between the two great music systems of the country. Days of a happy isolation and mutual exclusion are now gone. The Northern or Hindusthani system of music, it is well-known, has some of its own distinguishing features, such for instance as the following among others:—

(1) The *Shuddha* or foundation scale of the present Northern system is known as the Bilāval scale. That of the Southern system is called the Kanakāngi scale.

(2) To a general observer Hindusthani music will strike as mainly consisting of three important groups of *Rāgas, viz.,* (1) *Rāgas* taking *Ri* and *Dha Tivra;* (2) those taking *Ri* and *Dha Komal;* and (3) those taking *Ga* and *Ni Komala.*

(3) Every Hindusthani *Rāga* has its own *Vādi* or most prominent note, which is handled in a peculiar manner by the Northern artist.

(4) The *Rāgas* are divided into *Purva* and *Uttara* according to the position of the *Vādi note.*

(5) Stated times of the night and day are assigned to particular *Rāgas,* according to a design which might suggest a psycho-physiological basis.

(6) The *Tivra Madhyama* plays a very important part in the Hindusthani system. It not only facilitates the *Thāla* arrangement, but it enables the singer or listener to approximately determine the time of the *Rāga.*

(7) *Rāgas* fit to be sung at sunrise and sunset are known as *Sandhiprakāsha Rāgas.* These, as a general rule, belong to that group of *Rāgas* which take the *Ri* and *Dha Komal.*

(8) *Rāgas* which take *Ga* and *Ni Komal* usually come in the middle of the day and the middle of the night.

(9) *Rāgas* taking *Ri, Dha, Ga,* and *Ni Tivra* are usually sung immediately after the *Sandhiprakasha Rāgas.*

(10) An evening *Rāga* could easily be converted into a morning *Rāga* by changing the *Vādi* note thereof.

(11) The Northern musicians have their own ways of introducing the *Vivādi* notes into their *Rāgas.*

(12) The *Purva Rāgas* disclose their best charms in the *Aroha* or ascent, and the *Uttara Rāgas* do so in the descent or *Avaroha.*

(13) *Rāgas* immediately preceding the *Sandhiprakāsha,* that is to say, those which are sung in the third quarter of the day and the third quarter of the night usually prolong the notes *Sā, Ma,* and *Pa.* They will also be found to have one of these three notes for the *Vādi.*

(14) The evening *Sandhiprakāsha Rāgas,* as a general rule, do not omit both *Ga* and *Ni* altogether, and the morning *Sandhiprakāsha Rāgas* do not omit *Ri* and *Dha* altogether.

(15) The graces, flourishes and embellishments used by the Northern musicians are in many cases quite different to those used by the Southern musicians. The *Gamakas* of the Northern musicians differ from those of the Southern musicians.

(16) The *Alapa* singing of the Northerner is easily distinguishable from that of the Southerner.

(17) The conception of musical composition in the North differs from that of the South.

(18) There are several artistic *Rāga* mixtures permissible in the Northern system for which there will be no room in the Southern system.

(19) The *Tāla* system of Hindusthani music materially differs from that of the Karnataki music.

(20) The Northern musician would seem to sacrifice *Tāla* for the sake of his *Rāga,* whilst the Southern musician would seem to do the reverse.

I do not think it necessary to enumerate any more.

Here you might be tempted to ask the question, how are we to reconstruct a workable music system for the north on the *Skāstric* basis of the Southern *Granthas* ? I say that is very easily done. I think the valuable work of the Southern Pandit Vyankatmakhi will serve as an excellent model for us. I have already said that fortunately the twelve notes of the scale which the Southern writers use as the basis of their system are identically the same as those used by our Hindusthani musicians. Their principles of *Thāta* and *Rāga* construction are also the same as ours. There will be absolutely no harm, therefore, in accepting Vyankatmakhi's mathematically accurate 72 *Melakartas* or parent modes for our purposes together with the reasons which the Pandit assigns for their creation. His reasons are given in the 4th chapter called *Melaprakarnam* :—

ननु द्विसप्ततिर्मेला भवता परिकल्पिताः ॥80॥
प्रसिद्धाः पुनरेतेषु मेलाः कतिचिदेव हि ।
दृश्यंते न तु सर्वेऽपि तेन तत्कल्पनं बृथा ॥81॥
कल्पनागौरवन्यायादिति चेदिदमुच्यते ।

अनंताः खलु भेदास्ता देशस्था अपि मानवाः ।।82।।
तेषु सांगीतिकैरूच्चावचसंगीतकोविदैः ।
ये कल्पयिष्यमाणाश्च कल्प्यमानाश्च कल्पिताः ।।83।।
अस्मदादिभिरज्ञाता ये च शास्त्रैगोचराः ।
ये च देशीयरागास्तद्रागसामान्य मेलकाः ।।84।।
येनपन्तुवराल्याख्य कल्याणि प्रमुखा अपि ।
नानादेशीयरागास्तद्राग सामान्य मेलकाः ।।85।।
संग्रहीतुं समुन्नीता एते मेला द्विसप्ततिः ।
ततश्चैतेषु वैयर्थ्यशंका किं कारणं भवेत् ।।86।।

Pandit Vyankatmakhi is looked upon as a great authority in the Southern presidency. He was, no doubt, a very powerful writer. The way in which he tells his readers how it will be impossible to exceed the number of 72 *Melakartas* so long as the number of notes used is twelve only is rather interesting. He says:—

यदि कश्चिन्नदुर्नीतमेलेऽभ्यस्तद्विसप्ततेः।।81।।
न्यूनं वाऽप्यधिंक वापि प्रसिद्धैर्द्वादशस्वरैः।
कल्पयेन्मेलने तर्हि ममायासो वृथा भवेत्।।90।।
न हि तत्कल्पने भाललोचनोऽपि प्रगल्भते
तस्माद्यथैकपंचाशद्वर्णाः स्युर्मातृकामिधाः।।91।।
न हीयंते न वर्धंते तथा मेला द्विसप्ततिः।
एवं सामान्यतो मेलाः प्रोक्ताद्व्यधिकसप्तति।।92।।

Having taken these 72 *melas* as the exhaustive number of our parent modes for the Hindusthani music, we may take from Bhavabhatta's works the process of obtaining the mathematically possible number of *Odava, Shadava,* and *Sampurna Rāgas* derivable from each of the 72 modes. Bhavabhatta says :—

रागस्तु नवधा प्रोक्तः पूर्णःस्यात्सप्तभिःस्वरैः।
षड्िःभः षाडवसंज्ञः स्यादौडुवः पंचमिर्भवेत।।94।।
यथार्थनामकाः षट्स्युर्भेदा भावप्रभाषिताः।
पूर्णौडुवकसंज्ञस्तु पूर्णषाडवसंज्ञकः।
तथौडुवकपूर्णः स्यात्षाडवाद्यस्तु पूर्णकः।।95।।
षाडवौडुवकश्चापि तथौडुवकषाडवः।।
प्रोक्तो नवविधो रागः श्रीजनार्दन सूनुना ।।96।।

(*Anupa Sangita Vilāsa, Rāgādhyāya*)

Each *Mela* when so dealt with will give us the possible number of *Janya Rāgas* from it. We may select only such of the 72 *Thātas* as we think necessary for the classification thereunder of the *Rāgas* actually sung now in Northern India and then proceed to formulate the whole system.

You will thus see how it is quite possible, and easy too, to establish our current Hindusthani music on a sound foundation, and thereby to render its study perfectly easy. We may, at the same time, be able to retain every one of our special Northern characteristics and thereby keep our system easily distinguishable from the Southern system. I should select only some ten most popular *"melas"* (parent modes) out of the 72, and proceed to classify all our current *Rāgas* under them. Having finished the classification of the *Rāgas,* the next natural step would be to take each of these in order and write its detailed description and points of differentiation, not omitting to state side by side what all the available ancient authorities have had to say about the same.

Here you will naturally ask me, how is all that to be done and when and by whom ? I say, that all these things have already been attempted by me and the results of my labours have been embodied in a Sanskrit publication entitled the

"लक्ष्यसंगीतम्" *(Lakshya Sangitam).* This book has been written in the simplest Sanskrit style, and in order to make its contents perfectly accessible to those unacquainted with that language, I have written a copious commentary on it in Marathi, of which three volumes extending over something like 1,500 pages have already appeared. The book was written in the Sanskrit language not with any pedantic motives, nor with the intention of palming it off upon the reading public as a very old text, but in order to place it within the reach of all educated Indians in all parts of the country. This fact is patent upon a perusal of the title page of the publication itself. The book was published anonymously, in order to give the reading public more freedom of criticism than they would have liked to exercise if it were known to them that I was the author of it, as also to leave to myself some room to correct, in the commentary which I proposed to write on the text, such of the inaccuracies therein as may be brought to light by the unimpeded criticism. I may be permitted to mention here that these publications have been favourably reviewed in the local papers and are now fast getting into the favour of those who are competent to judge. In order to further popularize and put into circulation the rules of the differentiations of the various *Rāgas,* as well as the detailed descriptions of the modes of singing them, hundreds of ready made easy "सरगम" *(Sarigamas)* and "लक्षणगीत" *(Lakshanagitas)* embodying the same have been specially composed by me and placed in the market for sale at cost price so as to make them available to a large number of music students. In the construction of the *Gitas,* in order to make them true and reliable representations of the *Rāgas,* as at present sung, I used as models songs which I had learnt under the best of masters, making only such corrections, here and there, as were necessary. Many of these songs have become popular already, and it is a very hopeful sign of the times, that they have found favour with the professional classes too. Special students with good voices are being coached up by me for the purpose of being made into music teachers of the system recorded in the *Lakshyasangita* and its commentary, "The *Hindusthani Sangit Paddhati,*" and I earnestly hope that my humble, tentative, and disinterested labours of a lifetime in the cause of our great Hindusthani music towards making its study and instruction easy by systematising it, will bear fruit.

I shall now, with your permission, acquaint such of you as have not already read the books in question, with a brief but fairly exhaustive idea of the system formulated by me. You will agree with me that although innumerable pleasing combinations of notes are possible which will satisfy the essential conditions of a *Rāga,* our Hindusthani musicians are not heard to sing more than about two hundred different *Rāgas.* Taking these in hand, I draw upon the 72 possible parent modes or *Thātas* of Vyankatmakhi Pandit's work *Chaturdandiprakāshikā* (चतुर्दंडीप्रकाशिका) and selected only 10 of them, such as could be conveniently used as parent modes for our Hindusthani *Rāgas.* I may here mention to you, that the learned Pandit himself selected 19 of them for the classification of the Southern *Rāgas* of his time. The ten *Thātas* selected by me were the following :—

1.	शान्तकल्याण	यमन
2.	धीरशंकराभरण	बिलावल
3.	हरिकेदारगौव्व	खमाज
4.	मायामालवगौव्व	भैरव
5.	काशीरामक्रिया	पूर्वी
6.	गमकक्रिय	मारवा
7.	श्रीराग	काफी
8.	नारीरीतिगौल	आसावरी

9. जनीतोडि भैरवी

10. शैवपंतुवराली तोडी

I then classified all the *Rāgas* under one or the other of these ten *Thātas,* the principle of classification adopted being the affinity between the *Rāga* and the *Janak Thāta* to which it was allotted. Thus, for instance, *Rāgas* like *Hamir, Kedāra, Kamoda, Shyāma,* etc., and allied *Rāgas* showing a distinct affinity with the *Yamana Thāta* were allotted to that *Thata.* Likewise, *Shree, Jetāshri, Tanki, Puriā-Dhanashri, Mālavi, Gouri,* etc., have been allotted to the *Purvi Thāta,* while *Kālingada, Gunakri, Jogi, Rāmakali,* etc., have been placed under the *Bhairava Thāta.* The whole classification has been skilfully and concisely described in the following 11 *Shlokas* of the *Sangit Kalpadrumānkura,* which is an epitome of the *Lakshya Sangit,* and is the work of Pandit Appa Tulsi, a well-known Sangit Vidwan, in the employ of H. E. H. the Nizam, and a worthy collaborator of mine in the matter of systematisation of the music of Northern India. The eleven Shlokas referred to are :—

मेलाः स्युर्दश गीतिपद्धतिगताः कल्याणवेलावलः
खंमाजा ह्यथ भैरवस्तदनुगा भैरव्यथासावरीं ।
तोडी पूर्व्यथ मारवा बहुमता काफीति रागाः क्रिया-
सौकर्यादिह वैणिकैरमिहिताः श्रीशावतारा इव ।।1।।

मेले कल्याणनाम्नि प्रभवति यमनः शुद्धभूपौ हमीरः
श्यामच्छायानटोऽयं विलसत इह कामोदकेदारसंज्ञौ ।
हिंदोलो मालवश्रीस्तदनु यमनिका गौडसारंग एवं
प्रख्याताश्चंद्रकांतप्रभृतय इतरेऽप्यत्र वैजन्यरागाः ।।2।।

मेले वेलावलीये विहगककुभपाहाडिकादेशकाराः
शुक्ला नट्टोऽथ दुर्गा तदनु निगदिता देवगिर्येष माडः ।

सर्पर्दा शंकरोऽसावपिच गुणकरिर्नाम हंसध्वनिश्च
लच्छाशाखश्च हेमप्रभृतय इह संकीर्तिता जन्यरामाः।।3।।

खंमाजामिधमेलके सुमधुरा झिंझूटिका सोरटी
खंबावत्यथ देशकस्तिलककामोदोऽथ रागेश्वरी ।
दुर्गा चापि तिलंगिका जयजयावंती च नारायणी
गौंडोऽथो बडहंसकश्च कथिता नागस्वरावल्यपि ।।4।।।

मेले भैरवनामकेऽप्यथ कलिंगो मेघरंजन्यथो
सौराष्ट्री किल योगिनी गुणकली सा रामकेली पुनः ।
बंगालः शिवभैरवश्च ललितायुक्पंचमोऽहीरिका
गौरा चापि हिजेजकोऽप्यथ च सावेरी विभासादयः ।।5।।
मेले पूर्व्यभिधानके प्रकथिता गौरी च रेवा पुनः
मालव्यप्यथ सा त्रिवेण्यथ च जैतश्रीश्च टंकी तथा।
वासंती परजाभिधा प्रकथिता पूर्याधनाश्रीरथ
श्रीरागश्च विभासदीपकमुखा रागास्तदुत्पत्तिकाः।।6।।

मेलेऽस्मिन्मारवाख्ये श्रमदुरधिगमे पूरिया संमतेयम्
तत्रैवैषा प्रसिद्धा विलसति ललिता सोहनी मालिगौरा।
भंखारा साजगिर्यप्यथ तदनुवराटी च जैत्रो बिभासः
संत्यन्ये पंचमाद्यस्त्विह खलु बहवो भट्टिहारादयोऽपि।।7।।

काफी धान्यथ पीलुसैंधविधनाश्रीदेशिवागीश्वरी
सूहाभीमपलासिका च पटमंजर्यप्यथोऽड्डाणकः।
नीलांबर्यथ हंसकंकणिशहाणामेघमल्लारकाः
सुग्राही च हुसेनिनायकिबहारामध्यमाद्यादयः।।8।।

मेले चासावरीयेऽप्यतिरुचिरतरे जौनपूरी तथैव
गांधारो देवपूर्वस्तदनु च कथिता भैरवी सिंधुपूर्वा।
अड्डाणो देशिकेयं पुनरथदरबार्यं त्र कर्णाटसंज्ञ-
श्चैवं चान्ये खटाद्या दह किल बहवः कीर्तिता जन्यरागाः।।9।।

मेले भैरविकाव्हयेऽतिमधुरेऽस्मिन् मालकौशिस्तथा
भूपालोऽथ धनाश्रिका तदनु जंगूलोऽप्यथो मोटकी।
सामंतोऽपि च शूद्धपूर्वक दह प्रोक्तस्तथा झीलफो
रागाश्चात्र वसंतपूर्वकमुखार्याद्यास्तु जन्याः स्मृताः।।10।।

तोडीमेले तोडीभेदा बहवोऽपि गुर्जरीप्रमुखाः।
मित्रैकमूलतानी मेलं सार्थं वितन्वती नूनं।।11।।

In order to obviate the difficulties which Sanskrit as a language might put in the path of the majority of our music loving population, the same author has written a small book in Hindi called the *"Rāgachandrikā Sāra,"* which is virtually a translation of the *"Rāga Chandrikā"* in Sanskrit written by himself. Having thus framed the skeleton of a system, I next directed my attention to be differentiations between the various derivative *Rāgas,* and have recorded these briefly in the *"Lakshyasangit"* and at great length in the *"Hindusthani Sangit Paddhati"* with copious illustration, so as to enable any man of ordinary intelligence and the necessary patience and love of the subject to distinguish and to identify with a fair amount of accuracy and certainty each of the numerous derivative *Rāgas* falling under the various *Thātas.*

The differentiation was made as a rule by clearly setting down the essentials of each of the *Rāgas.* These are, as you all know:—

(1) Whether the *Rāga* is *Odava, Shādhava* or *Sampurna.*
(2) What is the proper time for singing the same.
(3) What notes it does not take, and in such cases whether, the omission is in the *"Āroha"* (ascent) or *"Avaroha"* (descent).
(4) What is the *Vādi* or predominant note of the *Rāga* and what is its *Samvādi.*

(5) How are the *Anuvādi* notes *(i.e.,* those other than the *Vādi* and *Samvādi* notes) to be utilised in the development of the *Rāga.*

(6) Whether the beauty of the *Rāga* lies in the *"Purvānga"* or the *"Uttarānga" (i.e.,* in the lower or the upper tetrachord), and then again whether in the *Āroha* or *Avaroha.*

(7) What mistakes are to be avoided in the singing of the *Rāgas.*

(8) Minute shades of difference between closely allied *Rāgas;* such as श्री and गौरी, जैताश्री and पूरियाधनाश्री, आसावरी and जौनपुरी, देशी and देवगांधार, त्रिवेणी and टंकी, मारवा and पूरिया, भठियार and भंखार, भैरव and रामकली, भीमपलासी and धनाश्री, काफी and सिंदूरा, बिहाग and शंकरा, देस and सोरट, etc.

Besides this, general directions were given as to the "प्रस्तार" (development) of the *Rāgas* by pointing out the ग्रह, अंश, न्यास, and विश्रांतिस्थान (halting places), as also the "पकड" or "catches" (specific combinations of notes which even when sung by themselves are enough to depict the *Rāga)* such as "नि, सा रे ग, मग" to express the "पूर्वी" *Rāga,* or the "सानिधनि," to indicate the "पुरिया" *Rāga* and so forth. Long illustrations are given to show the प्रस्तार and thereby to enable the student to sing and develop the *Rāga* with purity, beauty and grace.

In short, everything possible for me was done to record accurately, exhaustively and definitely the *Rāga,* as sung at the present day, while at the same time making its study and singing a matter of easy self-application. Thus, I have tried to redeem our music from the hands of the illiterate artists whose method of teaching is unscientific, inasmuch as unsystematic, and consequently unappealing and unacceptable to the educated student and also unnecessarily long and tedious and incapable of permanent results. A student of music who learns from the "लक्ष्यसंगीत" and the "हिंदुस्थानी संगीत पद्धति" teaches himself at least the firm and unshakable foundation of his music and the finishing, the picking up of graces and beauties, is done by merely listening to the singing of excellent practical artists when occasion offers ; for, the precise "स्वरज्ञान" which is insisted upon as an essential in every student of music by the *"Paddhati,"* and for which provision is made in the "स्वरमालिका" which is the Primer in my system of musical instruction, makes it possible for him to capture these graces and beauties on the wing.

The लक्ष्य संगीत *(Lakshya Sangit)* reads like a *"sutra"* book and its object is easy memorisation, and the same may be said of the books रागकल्पद्रुमांकुर, रागचंद्रिका and चंद्रिकासार. In order to give due currency to the system formulated by me in the Northern part of the country, which is the home of "Urdu" language, Thakur M. Nawab Ali Khan of Lucknow, a friend of mine and our President, who appreciated and wished to popularise my mode of classification, wrote a treatise in Urdu by name *"Marfat-ul-Naghmat,"* which embodies the same, and I am glad to say that work has already gone into a second and enlarged edition. In order to bring the system home to those who are not acquainted with either Sanskrit or Urdu other friends of mine put the first part of the *Paddhati* into the Gujerati language and the second and third parts are in the process of translation. It is with no small gratification that I learn now that my works have been able to attract attention also of the music lovers of the Southern part of the country.

Having thus attempted the systematisation of the music of Northern India on the basis of a single *Grāma*—the *Shadja Grāma*—and having tried the system by the test of public appreciation during these nine or ten years, I think I am in a position to say that the system is a fairly workable one and has done its best to give the necessary amount of stability to our Hindusthani music at a time when its state was getting far from satisfactory.

My object in laying all these facts before you is not to advertise myself or to blow my own trumpet, but simply to place before those who are competent to judge, my own handiwork for honest and dispassionate criticism, and I may assure you, that I, whose sole ambition in life has been to do my duty towards this art of arts in its degenerate condition, and not personal gain, who have always welcomed my critics and look upon them as my benefactors, still hold myself open to correction and suggestion, in view of the fact that all such criticism and suggestion are a contribution to the task I have undertaken.

The first step then in the work of the revival of our Northern music has been attempted by me and my labours have so far resulted in a fair measure of success. I feel happy at the thought that I have been able to mould a model for my successors to improve upon and to perfect; and I cannot but hope that in a few years more there will be an easy system for the instruction of our music, which will lend itself to mass education. Then will the ambition of India be fulfilled, for then the Indians will have music in the curricula of their Universities and music instruction will be common and universal. And if it please Providence to so dispense that there is a fusion between the two systems of the North and the South, then there will be a National music for the whole country and the last of our ambitions will be reached, for then the great Nation will sing *one* song. Once there is a system for music the gates of instruction will be thrown open and compulsory musical education will immediately follow almost as a natural consequence. Writing easy text-books and gradual manuals will be accomplished in a trice. Indeed, optimism in these matters is permissible, for I have very high hopes that the new Hindu University which has recently been established at Benares will have a faculty of music and thus the work of imparting education in music will travel fast.

My object in placing my system before this representative assembly has been to draw the attention of all these representatives to my imperfect model and to seek their help in perfecting it, with a view to facilitate the work of the University by having a system for our music ready when the University comes forward to ask for it.

Before concluding this address, I shall take this opportunity to express my immense gratitude to our noble and enlightened Prince and Ruler H. H. the Maharaja Saheb Gaekwar who takes such keen interest in the matter and has placed the whole of India under his obligation by his enabling us representatives to assemble here for this glorious work of the revival of our degenerate art, as also by taking the lead in acknowledging, by doing so, the incalculable value of musical education to humanity. It is my earnest hope that the fact of this value will also be acknowledged by the other Native Rulers in this country by their making common cause with this movement and by their inviting the Conference to assemble in the regions under their rule in future years and that by this co-ordination of efforts, the last goal of general mass education in Music will be attained.

With these words, Ladies and Gentlemen, I will conclude my address.

ॐ तत्सत्।

V. N. BHATKHANDE.